NEW DIRECTIONS FOR TEACHING AND LEAR.

Robert J. Menges, *Northwestern University*
EDITOR-IN-CHIEF

Marilla D. Svinicki, *University of Texas, Austin*
ASSOCIATE EDITOR

Honoring Exemplary Teaching

Marilla D. Svinicki
University of Texas, Austin

Robert J. Menges
Northwestern University

EDITORS

Number 65, Spring 1996

JOSSEY-BASS PUBLISHERS
San Francisco

HONORING EXEMPLARY TEACHING
Marilla D. Svinicki, Robert J. Menges (eds.)
New Directions for Teaching and Learning, no. 65
Robert J. Menges, Editor-in-Chief
Marilla D. Svinicki, Associate Editor

Microfilm copies of issues and articles are available in 16mm and 35mm,
as well as microfiche in 105mm, through University Microfilms Inc., 300
North Zeeb Road, Ann Arbor, Michigan 48106-1346.

ISSN 0271-0633   ISBN 0-7879-9979-2

NEW DIRECTIONS FOR TEACHING AND LEARNING is part of The Jossey-Bass
Higher and Adult Education Series and is published quarterly by Jossey-
Bass Inc., Publishers, 350 Sansome Street, San Francisco, California
94104-1342. Second-class postage paid at San Francisco, California, and
at additional mailing offices. POSTMASTER: Send address changes to New
Directions for Teaching and Learning, Jossey-Bass Inc., Publishers, 350
Sansome Street, San Francisco, California 94104-1342.

SUBSCRIPTIONS for 1996 cost $50.00 for individuals and $72.00 for institutions, agencies, and libraries.

EDITORIAL CORRESPONDENCE should be sent to the editor-in-chief, Robert J.
Menges, Northwestern University, Center for the Teaching Professions,
2003 Sheridan Road, Evanston, Illinois 60208-2610.

Cover photograph by Richard Blair/Color & Light © 1990.

TCF Manufactured in the United States of America on Lyons Falls
Pathfinder Tradebook. This paper is acid-free and 100 percent
totally chlorine-free.

CONTENTS

FROM THE SERIES EDITORS

About This Publication. Since 1980, *New Directions for Teaching and Learning* (*NDTL*) has brought a unique blend of theory, research, and practice to leaders in postsecondary education. *NDTL* sourcebooks strive not only for solid substance but also for timeliness, compactness, and accessibility.

The series has four goals: to inform readers about current and future directions in teaching and learning in postsecondary education, to illuminate the context that shapes these new directions, to illustrate these new directions through examples from real settings, and to propose ways in which these new directions can be incorporated into still other settings.

This publication reflects our view that teaching deserves respect as a high form of scholarship. We believe that significant scholarship is conducted not only by researchers who report results of empirical investigations but also by practitioners who share disciplined reflections about teaching. Contributors to *NDTL* approach questions of teaching and learning as seriously as they approach substantive questions in their own disciplines, and they deal not only with pedagogical issues but also with the intellectual and social context in which these issues arise. Authors deal on the one hand with theory and research and on the other with practice, and they translate from research and theory to practice and back again.

About This Volume. In the present issue, the authors address the question of how institutions can recognize and reward those faculty who go beyond mere competence and truly represent the best teaching higher education has to offer. Many standard processes are critiqued and innovations suggested for the honoring of exemplary teaching on a continuing basis. Many of these chapters grew out of the research program on faculty and instruction of the National Center on Postsecondary Teaching, Learning, and Assessment. Maryellen Weimer and Robert Menges of the National Center arranged with Clara Lovett of the American Association for Higher Education to program several sessions about exemplary teaching at the association's 1994 Forum on Faculty Roles and Rewards. Chapters by the following authors are based on presentations at that conference: Centra, Feldman, Forsythe and Gandolfo, Jenrette and Hays, Menges, Meyer and Penna, Smith and Walvoord, and Sorcinelli and Davis.

Robert J. Menges, *Editor-in-Chief*
Marilla D. Svinicki, *Associate Editor*

EDITORS' NOTES

Many colleges and universities are seeking ways to honor faculty who are out-standing teachers. Should such programs be widespread or highly selective? Based in the college or in the department? Small or large? Student-driven or faculty-driven? How should exemplary teachers be identified? What data can be relied upon to represent teachers' accomplishments? Data from students? From colleagues? From outsiders? These questions are addressed in this volume of *New Directions for Teaching and Learning*.

The chapters in this volume are divided into four parts. Authors in the first part (Chapters One through Four) consider varying formats for awards. In Chapter One, Robert Menges critically considers traditional awards, those given to a single teacher on a one-time basis. He discusses problems in this system and notes suspicions such awards raise about validity of the data used to identify recipients. In Chapter Two, Susan Kahn describes a much different system which recognizes departments rather than individuals and fosters cooperative efforts in teaching.

In Chapter Three, Hoke Smith and Barbara Walvoord suggest recognizing *all* individuals who achieve a high standard in their teaching, by employing a program that awards certification to those who excel. Nancy Chism, Jane Fraser, and Robert Arnold report in Chapter Four the results of a survey of institutions that have created academies of outstanding teachers, similar to the national disciplinary academies.

Authors in the second part of this volume (Chapter Five through Chapter Nine) look at the evidence and procedures used to identify exemplary teachers. In Chapter Five, Joseph Lowman lists characteristics of effective teachers that should be considered in any attempt to identify exemplars. Chapter Six, by Kenneth Feldman, and Chapter Seven, by John Centra, examine the validity and reliability of the most common evaluation data on teaching: data from students and from colleagues. These authors argue strongly that we can have reliable and valid data from several sources if we put aside our biases and look objectively at results. In Chapter Eight, Thomas Angelo suggests using sound evaluation practices to examine the many measures of teaching that have a good correlation with student learning. A final look at ways of documenting exemplary teaching is offered in Chapter Nine, by Laurie Richlin and Brenda Manning. Their discussion of the portfolio concept logically extends cautions mentioned in the previous chapter about the requirements of data sufficient for making good judgments.

The authors in Part Three (Chapter Ten through Chapter Fifteen) describe teaching award programs in different venues. Reading through these variations, one is struck by their many differences as well as by their similarities.

Part Four (Chapter Sixteen) highlights what can be gleaned from the previous chapters. We suggest ten guidelines that will help a new program to benefit from the successes while avoiding the pitfalls of those that have gone before. In the end, we recognize that each program has its own goals and constituencies and will therefore be unique.

This volume of *New Directions for Teaching and Learning* is a publication of the National Center on Postsecondary Teaching, Learning, and Assessment (NCTLA).

Work reported in several of the chapters was supported by NCTLA through funding to Pennsylvania State University from the Office of Educational Research and Improvement, U.S. Department of Education. The only federally funded national research and development center devoted specifically to postsecondary education, NCTLA is a consortium housed at Pennsylvania State University. Its members are the University of Illinois, the University of Chicago, Arizona State University, Syracuse University, Northwestern University, and the University of Southern California. The findings and opinions expressed in these chapters are solely those of the authors.

Marilla D. Svinicki
Robert J. Menges
Editors

MARILLA D. SVINICKI is director, Center for Teaching Effectiveness, University of Texas, Austin.

ROBERT J. MENGES is professor of education and social policy, Northwestern University, and senior researcher, National Center on Postsecondary Teaching, Learning, and Assessment.

Problems common to awards programs can be avoided by subjecting them to three tests of program effectiveness.

Awards to Individuals

Robert J. Menges

Awards that honor exemplary teaching have proliferated across the landscape of higher education. According to *Campus Trends 1993* (El-Khawas, 1993), seven in ten institutions in 1993 reported giving annual awards to recognize outstanding teaching, a sizable increase from 1987 when the proportion was about half. Institutions reported that they recognized teaching through ceremonies (69 percent), special funds (40 percent), and released time (26 percent). An increase to salary in recognition of outstanding teaching was reported by 45 percent, an unfortunate decline of 6 percent from 1987.

Programs to honor exemplary teaching typically spring from laudable purposes, the most important being to raise the esteem in which teaching is held. Programs are expected to prompt greater support for higher education from constituencies outside our institutions and, by energizing faculty, to improve the quality of teaching and learning within those institutions. But despite praiseworthy purposes, awards programs often fall short in practice. Their benefits are sometimes offset by unintended negative consequences.

The focus of this chapter is on problems that occur in the most common approach to teaching awards—institution-based awards to individual faculty who have demonstrated noteworthy accomplishments as teachers. I discuss five problems often encountered in these programs. I then introduce three tests that such programs should meet if they are to be considered effective. Finally, I suggest some questions for determining how well a program meets those tests.

Common Problems for Award Programs

Selection Procedures and Criteria. The aspect of *selection* I wish to emphasize concerns the tension between secrecy and openness. Often, selection

NEW DIRECTIONS FOR TEACHING AND LEARNING, no. 65, Spring 1996 © Jossey-Bass Publishers

procedures are poorly understood by faculty, and selection criteria are vague. As a result, suspicions about the integrity of the program arise.

Undoubtedly advantages do flow from confidential deliberations and somewhat ambiguous selection criteria. On the one hand, criticism of those who are honored will be minimized. It is difficult to criticize ends when the means are unclear. On the other hand, vagueness and secrecy make it difficult for faculty to figure out how the program operates, to estimate their chances of success, and to prepare applications likely to be selected.

Vagueness and secrecy foster suspicions about the objectivity and accuracy of the selection process. In the first year of one university's award program, for example, all the awards went to white males, and in the second year, none of the awards went to white males. Faculty were understandably concerned about possible bias. Because no information was available regarding the pool of nominees, speculation soon fed suspicions about the fairness of selection procedures.

Many faculty share these concerns. In one of the studies at the National Center on Postsecondary Teaching, Learning, and Assessment, Jennifer Quinn examined information from award winners at several research universities and from honored professors attending a forum on exemplary teaching supported by the American Association for Higher Education (Quinn, 1994). A significant number of these individuals, all of whom had been recognized for their interest and achievements in teaching, expressed reservations about the fairness of award programs. Among their suggestions for improvement were making criteria more specific and procedures more open.

Attaining clear selection criteria and ensuring inclusiveness is made more difficult by the diversity of academic disciplines and programs, the variety of settings in which faculty teach, and the varied instructional styles that faculty employ. Comparing the work of, say, teachers in the humanities with those in the performing arts, in languages, in the sciences, and in other fields is indeed complex, but it cannot be avoided.

Not only must awards programs comprehend the diversity of fields and settings and teaching styles but they also require fine distinctions among persons, all of whom are at very high levels of achievement. Awards programs rarely specify procedures for making such fine discriminations.

Once decisions have been made, results are typically communicated with little explanation. The selection committee for one program, for example, informed applicants who had not been chosen for an award that "all nominees were seen as uniformly excellent." Lack of feedback about differences between nominees who prevail and those who do not prevail leaves future applicants unclear about what is valued and unenthusiastic about the program.

In the absence of meaningful and useful information about selection procedures and criteria, faculty sometimes adopt the strategy of "passing the awards around." Thus, each unit or person within a unit feels assured of sooner or later receiving an award. Under those circumstances, complaints about unfair criteria are unlikely because no criteria of quality are actually applied.

Bias Toward Popularity. Bias other than racial and gender prejudice is sometimes imputed to teaching awards programs. I think particularly about the complaint that awards reflect popularity. More precisely, this is bias toward teaching as performance, the suspicion that awards favor polished presenters who teach large classes.

Awards are especially vulnerable to this criticism when students have a strong voice in selection. While it is difficult to imagine a defensible awards program without student input, the nature of that input deserves scrutiny. Student input is heavily influenced by the number of students taught. It tends to focus on what goes on in classrooms, which is visible and interesting, and to ignore how well teachers go about more mundane but less visible instructional tasks such as preparing for class and assessing student work. It tends to rely on end-of-course surveys, which are readily available but which may not provide information that is most relevant. Survey questions typically reflect conventional teacher-centered approaches that are consistent with the popularity stereotype. An innovative risk-taking teacher may actually be penalized by conventionally structured student evaluations.

Selection criteria and procedures should reflect the complexity of instructional tasks and settings even though doing so complicates selection procedures. That will go a long way toward countering the charge of bias toward popular performers.

Competition Versus Collaboration. When awards go to individuals, they reinforce competition rather than reward collaboration among faculty. Such awards define teaching as an individual activity. They require that one person or several persons win while all others lose.

The issue of competition arose in the Disney Channel's American Teacher Awards. These awards are bestowed annually upon elementary and secondary teachers after a nationwide search. Nominees are flown to Florida for the finals, where they appear on a live telecast produced by the Disney Channel. By the end of the week, one of the finalists prevails and is named the teacher of the year. The 1992 winner's acceptance speech took note of the discomfort he felt in displacing the others. He said that *all* the finalists deserved awards, and their experience of sharing was violated when only one could prevail as winner.

The win/lose requirement is especially counterproductive in settings where teamwork and cooperation are valued. We need to find ways to honor exemplary teaching by rewarding not just competition but also collaboration.

Questionable Incentives. Awards are intended to serve as incentives for faculty to value teaching and to devote time and energy to improving it. But if awards are to be effective, they must have certain characteristics. An effective incentive is future oriented, it is perceived as highly valuable, it is moderately difficult to attain, but it is realistically available. Unfortunately, typical teaching awards rarely meet these incentive conditions.

First, awards are not future oriented; instead, they celebrate past accomplishments rather then enabling future attainments. Second, faculty may not perceive awards as highly valuable. Awards are likely to be uniform, that is, all recipients receive the same "prize." Yet the incentive value of any prize, of course, is not uniform across recipients. People vary a great deal in what they find optimally rewarding. Third, teaching awards may be seen as requiring considerable effort, perhaps more than they are worth. To reach the level of teaching quality that makes me competitive, how much energy must I expend? Would comparable effort produce more valuable results if directed toward, say, an additional publication? An effective incentive should require a significant stretch, but it should not, obviously, exceed one's grasp. Teaching awards may be seen by most faculty as requiring a level of quality and an amount of effort that are beyond their grasp. Finally, if awards are to be effective incentives, they must be sufficiently plentiful. These four conditions of effective incentives, when applied to award programs, may point the way to significant improvements.

Special Awards Replacing Continuing Rewards. A college or university seeking to elevate the importance of teaching may be tempted to focus its commitment primarily around the awards it bestows. Awards may lead to premature satisfaction about the institution's attention to teaching. This self-satisfaction becomes particularly insidious when, even as teaching awards programs prosper, teachers' compensation fails to increase or is based on criteria that fail to reflect teaching effectiveness.

Research by Fairweather (1993) confirms suspicions that teacher productivity has little relationship to compensation. In studies for the National Center on Postsecondary Teaching, Learning, and Assessment, he found that professors who are paid most, even at institutions whose missions explicitly emphasize teaching, are those who publish, who obtain research grants, and who teach fewer and smaller classes. If we are to persuade parents, trustees, and legislators that colleges and universities do hold teaching in high esteem, we must alter this negative relationship between teaching and compensation.

When the award is a one-time cash payment, its value is almost always less than the adjustment to base salary that typically follows outstanding scholarly achievements or other professional recognition. As Kimball (1988) points out, an award of $1,000 invested at 5 percent interest will grow to a little over $2,500 in twenty years, whereas a 4 percent increment in a $25,000 salary, depending on future raises and retirement contributions, could come close to $60,000 in additional income over the same period. The ratio, he notes, is about twenty-four to one.

Programs of awards to individuals may be seen as an inexpensive way to satisfy an institution's commitment to honor teaching. At the universities studied by Quinn (1994), the total cost of awards was typically only a few thousand dollars per year. In even hard-pressed budgets, resources can usually be found to reap the considerable public relations benefits that awards programs bring.

Although public relations benefits of programs can be sizable, it is difficult to document other positive consequences. In a survey of award recipients at the University of California, Berkeley, more than 70 percent indicated that the award had very little or no positive effect on their advancement, either for promotion or salary (Schwartz, 1992).

The danger is that teaching awards will deflect attention from other strategies, especially salary increments, by which institutions demonstrate commitment to teaching. An awards program does not excuse institutions from weighing teaching appropriately in the faculty reward system.

Tests of an Effective Awards Programs

If a teaching awards program is effective, it will pass three tests. I call them the selection validity test, the faculty motivation test, and the test of public perceptions.

The selection validity test requires that those who receive awards be, in fact, the best teachers. The faculty motivation test requires that, as a result of the awards program, faculty devote greater effort to the quality of their teaching and to improving student learning. The test of public perceptions requires that, as a result of the program, external constituencies such as parents, community leaders, trustees, and legislators perceive that teaching is held in high esteem at the institution.

Programs that meet these tests have found ways to solve or avoid the problems enumerated above. Here are some questions to ask in assessing how well a program meets each of these tests.

Selection Validity Test. The selection validity test asks to what extent the program does what it claims to do, that is, how well does it select from all the eligible teachers those who are truly exemplary. This test has two dimensions: accuracy and representativeness.

Accurate selection

Does the program reflect core values of the institution? For example, if setting high expectations for students is a core value, how is that value reflected in the program? If collaboration among faculty is valued at the institution, how is that value reconciled with a program that is inherently competitive?

Are selection criteria and procedures generally known by faculty? Is there consensus that they are "correct"?

Does selection utilize information of various types (both qualitative and quantitative) and information from several sources?

Are nominees considered not only in light of their past accomplishments but also in light of their teaching plans for the future?

How confident are those who make selections that recipients are demonstrably superior in terms of program criteria?

Representativeness

Do recipients fairly represent the variety of fields (disciplines and other programs of study) and instructional situations (seminar, lab, studio, clinic, lecture hall)?

Do recipients fairly represent the variety of instructional activities that faculty perform (both in class and out)?

Is the program free of gender and ethnic biases?

Faculty Motivation Test. A successful program to honor exemplary teaching will energize faculty, making them more attentive to their teaching and its impact. This should be apparent to students and colleagues, and it should be evident more generally in the climate of the institution. The first four questions below deal with ways that programs can ensure the incentive value of awards, and the remainder suggest evidence for increased faculty motivation.

Ensuring Incentive Value
Are awards sufficiently numerous to encourage qualified faculty to apply?
Can each recipient choose from a menu of awards what is personally most valuable?
Is the value of the award at least as great as the effort required to obtain it?
Do unsuccessful applicants receive information about how their applications could be strengthened?

Evidence of Increasing Motivation
Are application rates increasing? Is there clamor for expansion of the program?
Do recipients report positive experiences in the wake of receiving the award?
Is there evidence that informal conversation about teaching has increased and become more thoughtful?
Do more teaching-related items appear on agendas of departmental and committee meetings?
Are instructional experiments and innovations more common?
Have student course and teacher evaluations become more positive?

Test of Public Perceptions. This test seeks evidence that external audiences have increased appreciation that teaching is valued and rewarded at the institution and that the quality of teaching and learning has improved.

Is media coverage about teaching more extensive and more positive?
When prospective students and their parents ask about teaching and programs of study, are their questions answered more readily?
When legislators ask about such matters as faculty workload, are their questions better informed?
Has external funding for the support of instructional innovation increased?

All these questions are influenced by many factors other than teaching awards program, but all of them deserve attention in designing programs intended to honor exemplary teaching.

Conclusion

Perhaps the primary conclusion we can draw from this discussion of individual awards is that awards programs cannot stand alone and apart. They should be consciously designed components of a larger effort at defining and recognizing teaching in all its forms and levels.

References

El-Khawas, E. *Campus Trends 1993*. Higher Education Panel Report No. 83. Washington, D.C.: American Council on Education, 1993.

Fairweather, J. S. "Academic Values and Faculty Rewards." *Review of Higher Education*, 1993, *17*, 43–68.

Kimball, B. *Teaching Undergraduates*. Buffalo, N.Y.: Prometheus, 1988.

Quinn, J. W. "Teaching Award Recipients' Perceptions of Teaching Award Programs." Paper presented at the Second AAHE Forum on Faculty Roles and Rewards, New Orleans, Jan. 1994.

Schwartz, C. "Is Good Teaching Rewarded at Berkeley?" *College Teaching*, 1992, *40* (1), 33–36.

ROBERT J. MENGES is professor of education and social policy, Northwestern University, and senior researcher, National Center on Postsecondary Teaching, Learning, and Assessment.

The rationale, history, and guidelines of the University of Wisconsin System's teaching award for academic departments and programs serves as a model for other institutions seeking ways to reward group teaching achievements.

Awards to Groups: The University of Wisconsin System's Departmental Teaching Award

Susan Kahn

Three years ago, the University of Wisconsin System (UW System) instituted the Regents Teaching Excellence Awards to increase the visibility and prestige of distinguished teaching in the system. Originally conceived along traditional lines as an award for outstanding individual teaching, the award program expanded in the following year to include a second, less traditional category: an award honoring an academic department or program that promotes and achieves excellence in teaching. Currently the board of regents annually honors two individual faculty members and one academic department or program in the UW System with awards of $5,000 each making it one of just a few institutions nationally that offer a department-level teaching award.

Background

The award was created as a result of a confluence of factors. First, the board of regents was seeking an alternative use of regent-donated funds from a discontinued program. Second, the board had been involved in several broad initiatives aimed at improving undergraduate teaching, learning, and curricula. A board-sponsored teaching award seemed an appropriate signal, at least symbolically, of their commitment to the university's teaching and learning mission. Third, the system administration, along with a number of faculty members and administrators from system institutions, had begun discussing alternative paradigms of scholarship, the nature of faculty work, and the rewards and incentives for such work and was seeking ways to translate these discussions into programmatic forms.

Help, inspiration, and catalysts to action came primarily from two sources: the American Association for Higher Education (AAHE) and the Association for American Colleges and Universities (AAC&U). In early 1993, AAHE sponsored the Faculty Roles and Rewards Conference, the first of a series of conferences on that topic. That conference identified as a major issue "shifting the focus of evaluation and accountability from individual faculty to groups of faculty, especially academic departments" (Edgerton, 1993, p. 23). Similarly, several studies by AAC&U stressed the importance of departmental collaboration on teaching and curriculum planning to the coherence of students' educational experience and overall intellectual growth and development in their undergraduate years. One study, *The Challenge of Connecting Learning,* called on faculty and departments to work collaboratively on "translating these common commitments [to students and teaching] into institutional practices and structure . . . supported by visible and concrete rewards" (1991, p. 21).

As these discussions unfolded, the UW System began to plan and move forward with several initiatives focused on the departments' crucial role in creating academic cultures that value and reward teaching. These initiatives included an annual systemwide institute for new department chairs and an ambitious systemwide project on faculty roles and rewards, led by the system's Undergraduate Teaching Improvement Council (UTIC) and linked to AAHE's national project on the role of the academic department.

It was within this context that the Regents Teaching Excellence Award for Academic Departments/Programs was launched, at the behest of then-Senior Vice President for Academic Affairs Stephen R. Portch. UTIC members, who represent all fifteen UW institutions, were charged with responsibility for developing criteria and guidelines for the award.

Criteria and Evidence

The guidelines that resulted from this process identified four main categories of evidence for examination by the award committee: recognizing and fostering excellence in teaching; approaching teaching as a public collaborative activity; thoughtfully constructing effective curricula for an academic program; and demonstrating a positive climate for significant impact on student learning.

For each of these four areas, the guidelines provide examples of kinds of evidence that might be appropriate and persuasive. The potential evidence includes documentation that teaching is supported through teaching-focused programs for new faculty, personnel policies and actions, and collaborative activities such as peer review and team teaching; documentation of curriculum-planning procedures; and most important, documentation by and about students—for example, student evaluations; results of efforts to assess student learning; and data on student enrollment, retention, and postgraduate experiences. In effect, the documentation constitutes a kind of departmental teaching portfolio that includes evidence for the four main areas of consideration; a departmental statement of teaching philosophy, goals, and strategies; and letters of support from current and former students.

Review Process

The selection and review process begins in December or January, when the UW System president invites each system institution to submit a nomination for the award. Institutions determine their own nomination procedures, which vary accordingly. On some campuses, for example, the chancellor or provost selects a department or program with a strong reputation for teaching excellence. At others, individual schools and colleges are asked to submit nominations, and a campuswide committee selects the institution's nominee.

Once at the system level, the selection and award process, administered by UTIC, has three stages. First, a screening committee made up of Office of Academic Affairs staff—most of whom are former or current faculty members—selects several finalists from among the nominees. Nomination materials for the finalists are then submitted to a special board of regents committee, which makes the final decision on that year's award recipient (part of the purpose in instituting the Regents Teaching Excellence Awards was to further educate regents about outstanding UW teachers, departments, and programs). Finally, at a summer or early fall board of regents meeting, the award-winning department or program is honored and the award presented.

Now in its third year, the program has attracted fairly good participation, with the number of nominations increasing each year. The quality and consistency of the supporting documentation have also improved noticeably.

Award Winners

The award recipients in the first two years of the program were a science department and an interdisciplinary program. The 1993 winner, the Department of Chemistry at the University of Wisconsin, Eau Claire, assembled an exceptionally persuasive portfolio that focused on a particular aspect of the department's undergraduate chemistry major—an extensive program of collaborative faculty and student research that has helped place the university among the top public undergraduate institutions nationally for production of chemistry graduates who go on to earn Ph.D.'s. In its teaching philosophy statement, the department argued that "in our environment, research invariably enhances teaching," and that "independent pursuit of a scholarly project by a student and the resulting one-to-one contact with faculty is one of the most effective teaching venues that can be provided."

Powerfully bolstering the department's case were impressive statistics on graduate school, professional school, and employment placements; on students' success in competing for national scholarships and awards; and on steady growth in the number and percentage of women chemistry graduates over the history of the program. Shortly before being nominated for the award, the department had been featured as a national model for effective science education in Sheila Tobias's book, *Revitalizing Undergraduate Science: Why Some Things Work and Most Don't* (1992). Additional external recognition had come in the form of a half-million dollar grant from Research Corporation that singled out UW-Eau Claire's undergraduate chemistry program as one of the nation's best and used it as a model for science programs at public undergraduate universities nationwide.

The 1994 award recipient, the Human Development Program at University of Wisconsin, Green Bay, took a different approach in its portfolio, giving relatively equal attention to addressing all four categories of evidence. UW-Green Bay is organized around interdisciplinary programs of study that function much as traditional disciplinary departments do at other institutions. The Human Development Program draws on such disciplines as biology, psychology, anthropology, and sociology to provide students with an understanding of (in the words of their application) "changes, tasks, and crises that occur throughout the life span" and of "factors and cultural contexts that promote normal development and deviations from normal development." Graduates go on to careers and postgraduate study in such areas as social services, health-related fields, and teaching.

As an interdisciplinary program, the Human Development Program clearly needed to demonstrate the coherence and effectiveness of its curriculum. It did so by showing how program faculty identified specific educational goals then designed a tightly conceptualized and rigorously assessed program around those goals. The program is distinguished by its extensive sponsorship of individualized learning experiences, such as internships, independent studies, and undergraduate research, and by its strong assessment program, which targets students at every level, from newly declared majors through alumni.

Persuasive arguments and evidence for a departmental commitment to teaching as a collective responsibility, undergraduate advising shared by all department members, and recognition of teaching achievement in personnel decisions further strengthened the Human Development Program's portfolio. So did a series of compelling letters from current and former students, a summary of assessment results and of highlights from a recent alumni survey, and strong statistics on postgraduate employment and study. In short, the nomination materials presented an excellent case for the program as a community of teacher-scholars dedicated to helping undergraduate students succeed through a well-focused, innovative, and effective course of study.

Impact

After only a few years of award program experience and just two award winners to date, any assessment of the Regents Teaching Excellence Award for Departments/Programs must necessarily be limited. However, I interviewed the chairs of the two winning departments as well as the chairs of several other nominated departments, and based on this limited sample, I offer the following tentative comments about the program's value and impact.

All the chairs agreed that the process of working with colleagues to prepare the nomination portfolio, and particularly to formulate a succinct statement on the department's teaching philosophy and goals, was in itself a valuable and informative exercise. The chairs felt also that the message conveyed in the award guidelines that departments are expected to work collaboratively and to *have* a philosophy of teaching was an important one.

The chairs of the two award-winning departments said the award had generated considerable local publicity, helped increase community awareness of the quality of their institutions, and served as a strong morale booster to their departments and campuses. Both departments had found the award helpful in student recruitment; the Department of Chemistry at UW-Eau Claire had used it in recruiting potential faculty members as well. The department chair noted that the award had confirmed the value of the faculty–undergraduate student research model that the department had developed. The UW-Green Bay Human Development Program chair agreed that the award sent a message that the department and institution were "good on their own terms"—and did not need to model themselves on research institutions in order to be recognized for their accomplishments.

At another level, those of us involved with administering the program and helping to select recipients have learned a great deal about work being done in exemplary departments across our university system. But it has also become clear that institutions of higher education largely lack well-developed approaches to documenting the impact of an entire program of study on students' mastery of a field and overall intellectual growth. Where such approaches do exist—for example, multiple holistic assessments conducted at several stages of students' academic careers—they are not yet as widely used nor as well defined as they might be.

Conclusion

Further development and wider use of strategies for assessing the quality of teaching and learning across departments or other units may be one key to improving the reward system for group teaching performance. We certainly hope that our Regents Teaching Excellence Award for Departments/Programs, in combination with other systemwide initiatives on faculty development, roles, and rewards, will serve as an incentive to such development and as a foundation for enhanced group rewards for teaching at institutions throughout the UW System.

References

The Challenge of Connecting Learning. Washington, D.C.: Association of American Colleges, 1991.

Edgerton, R. "The Re-Examination of Faculty Priorities." *Change,* 1993, 25 (4), 10–25.

Tobias, S. *Revitalizing Undergraduate Science: Why Some Things Work and Most Don't.* Tucson, Ariz.: Research Corp., 1992.

SUSAN KAHN is director of the University of Wisconsin System's Undergraduate Teaching Improvement Council and senior academic planner in the Office of Academic Affairs.

Can higher education benefit by honoring excellent teachers through certification? The positives and negatives are explored.

The "Certification" Paradigm

Hoke Smith, Barbara Walvoord

For years, supporters of teaching have attempted to attack the dominance of faculty research in determining who gets faculty rewards in higher education. Despite efforts that have included local and national teaching awards, the doctor of arts degree in teaching, the redefinition of scholarship, and more recently, legislative action, "publish or perish" is alive and well. These efforts have not established a reward system that weights teaching strongly in initial salary or hiring decisions. Until a competitive market rewards teaching on a par with research, the faculty reward system will remain dominated by the research paradigm. It is by addressing this problem of the market that the certification paradigm most strongly distinguishes itself from other paradigms.

Certification Defined

In the certification paradigm, individuals receive certification by meeting predetermined criteria. The word *certification* in this context means not "license to practice" but "mark of distinction given to those who meet particular standards."

We are aware of three certification programs currently being proposed or implemented in education. The first is the National Board for Professional Teaching Standards' scheme of voluntary certification for K-12 teachers, which is currently being implemented. The second is a program of the American Association of Colleges of Pharmacy (see Chapter Fifteen). A third, not yet implemented, is contained in our proposal, published in the *AAHE Bulletin,* for a national certification in higher education (Smith and Walvoord, 1993). This chapter explores the issues, strengths, and weaknesses in the paradigm.

New Directions for Teaching and Learning, no. 65, Spring 1996 © Jossey-Bass Publishers

Creating a National Market for Teaching

We have organized this discussion around the implications of six things that a certification system must do to create a national market for teaching in higher education. The system must (1) effectively balance supply and demand; (2) be criterion-referenced, that is, given to all who meet the stated criteria; (3) choose criteria that command the confidence of the community; (4) be known throughout the market in which a given faculty member will operate; (5) protect academic freedom; and (6) provide a visible mark of distinction for faculty. Inherent within each of these conditions are thorny issues.

Implications of Balanced Supply and Demand. If a certificate is to become coin of the realm in a national market, there must be a supply and a demand for it.

Supply. Single teaching awards cannot support a national market for award winners because these awards do not create a large enough supply of winners: typically, awards are competitive, resulting in only one or at most a few winners. Thus, on the one hand, if less than 20 percent of teachers earn certificates, certification will be a mark of prestige but will also remain little known—not something search committees will look for. On the other hand, if standards are set so that 20 to 60 percent of teachers earn certificates, search committees probably will begin asking for certification regularly, and many teachers will be motivated to work toward it. If more than 75 percent can earn certification, however, there is the risk that schools will begin to require rather than seek it, prefer it, and reward it. The fear that certification will become a necessity for everyone has been raised in every discussion we have had about the paradigm.

Demand. The certification system depends upon the assumption that if 20 to 60 percent of faculty held certification for excellence in teaching, schools would want and woo those certified teachers. Our own American Association for Higher Education (AAHE) proposal has argued this point on two bases: first, we noted how much publicity Hope College in Holland, Michigan (where one of us is an alumna), gleaned when one of its faculty won the national Council for the Advancement and Support of Education award for excellence in teaching; the college's hunger for external recognition of its excellence in teaching was very clear.

Second, we noted how institutions seek and use external recognition of faculty research: we used as an example a banquet for donors, board members, and legislators we attended at a major research university. The president bragged about the school's millions in grants, the listing of particular departments among the top ten or top twenty-five in the nation, and other external affirmations of excellence in research but said not one word about excellence in teaching—and what could he have said? There are few if any external affirmations of institutional excellence in teaching. The existence of a nationally recognized teaching certificate would allow an institution to brag about its percentage of certified teachers the same way it brags about its research.

But the basis of that brag must be sound. If the basis is simply the percentage of total faculty certified, each institution will hire as many certified faculty as possible and help its current faculty get certified. It might not distinguish between a teacher who taught ten graduate students and a teacher who taught one hundred (or many more) undergraduates. Further, unless the certification extended to adjuncts and teaching assistants, a university might brag that 100 percent of its "faculty" were certified but still have 75 percent of its students taught by uncertified teaching assistants and adjuncts. A better statistic would be the *number of student credit hours generated by certified teachers,* or the *percentage of students taught by certified teachers.*

Implications of Criterion-Referenced Certification. In order to create a market, certification must be criterion-referenced—that is, given to all who meet the announced criteria, rather than to those who outperform their peers. Explicit criteria must be widely and consistently understood and applied. Both teachers and schools must have reasonable confidence that the certificate means the same thing in any institution. Current awards, in contrast, often are competitive; winning depends upon the quality of the other applicants. Judges may read and rank the applications without fully stating the judging criteria.

If criteria remain tacit and judges rank applications competitively, then the whole enterprise depends on judges who are trusted by the community. In fact, one weakness of teaching awards is that if judges are perceived to be biased or inexpert, the credibility of the award is destroyed. In the certification paradigm, trust is transferred in part from the judges to a statement of criteria.

Specifying the criteria for the certificate has other implications. If criteria are well known, faculty could work toward them with some expectation of reward. This motivational power is one of the strong advantages of the certification paradigm.

Stating the criteria could also be a powerful force in teacher and teaching assistant training. It could shape graduate education, since graduate programs presumably would help their teaching assistants achieve "apprentice certification." The criteria would also drive faculty development, as campuses helped their faculty achieve certification.

Implications of the Criteria Chosen. Like coins, certification will work only if buyers and sellers have faith in the currency. Thus, standards for certification must be developed in a highly public forum so the certificate can be recognized as representing widely accepted standards.

One method for assuring wide credibility would be to base the criteria upon the results of research that has sought to establish the teaching practices most likely to enhance student learning (summarized, for example, in Chickering and Gamson, 1987, and Kurfiss, 1987). If high-stakes certification is based on that research, the research methodology and epistemology will come under increasing scrutiny, another desirable result.

Another proof of teaching excellence would be a direct measure of student outcomes from each teacher's class. This is an expensive and difficult proposition. Moreover, there will be hot debate over any attempt to use student outcomes as a basis for teacher certification, given that many things beyond a teacher's control can affect what students learn. But there will also be hot debate over any teacher certification that does *not* include student outcomes.

The bottom line is that what is good teaching and how can it be measured are not easy questions to answer. If higher education waits for the perfect instrument to measure teaching, a market for certification will never materialize. If a national board of experts were engaged to propose criteria and if high stakes were involved, the research would follow, and the resulting rich discussion might be one of the most valuable outcomes of the certification debate.

Implications of Being Known in the Market. A certification system must extend throughout the market in which any given faculty member operates. Every search committee must know about certification and look for it. After our proposal appeared in the *AAHE Bulletin,* a statewide committee in Ohio debated whether Ohio by itself could establish such a system. They decided that it could not. Since many Ohio faculty operate in a national rather than a state job market, a state certification system could not fulfill the market purpose we had envisioned for national certification.

If a certification system is to be phased in, it makes more sense to do it by disciplines, since most faculty identify strongly with their discipline. In higher education, the action of the pharmaceutical educators to certify master teachers (see Chapter Fifteen) is thus a very important development. It may serve as a pilot for a larger certification system.

The pharmaceutical educators' model also suggests that perhaps, rather than being operated as a centrally organized system, higher education certification might be run entirely by the disciplinary societies as separate entities. Each discipline could establish teaching standards just as they produce other professional standards.

What remains clear is that, to be effective, standards must be widely accepted, widely known, and widely trusted in all the arenas where a given faculty member might seek employment or promotion.

Implications for Academic Freedom. Certification raises concerns about academic freedom. A narrow response would remind faculty that academic freedom does not prohibit teachers from being recognized for excellence in the facilitation of student learning. But that argument probably begs the larger issue that faculty seem to feel in their bones and to label "academic freedom." One component of that bone-deep feeling is that faculty see certification as another battle in the larger struggle to retain autonomy in the face of increasingly managerial administrations and centralized educational systems (see Bergquist, 1992).

One way to have a certification system and still protect faculty autonomy would be to have the system controlled by faculty, a self-regulating measure that might well stave off more centralized attempts by boards, legislators, and administrators to impose certification or other modes of accountability.

However, faculty concern about academic freedom has another basis: faculty fear that establishing criteria applicable to all teachers will narrow the definition of "good teaching" and disenfranchise the wonderfully varied, creative, and often eccentric teachers, the ones people frequently remember with gratitude and affection. Faculty are afraid that a rigid specification of scientifically derived strategies of good teaching will take the intuitive juices out of the act and constrain the special synergy that develops between teacher and students. Care will have to be taken that teaching is not cast into a rigid straightjacket at a time when flexibility may be needed to meet changing conditions in the classroom.

Further, teachers sometimes wonder whether a national certification system, no matter how well administered, how teacher controlled, and how restrained and disciplined at first, could at some point be the instrument of a demagogue. For example, would a teacher certification system have helped the McCarthyites or checked them? To such fears, certification proponents answer with all the safeguards and flexibility they can devise.

One possible avenue toward safety and flexibility would be to decentralize the certification process. (For example, the professional societies could manage certification for teaching in their disciplines, as mentioned earlier.) Another avenue would be to keep the criteria and process of application and evaluation always in faculty hands and to ensure that the process of choosing the teachers who make the judgments and set the criteria is democratic, fair, and eclectic. Educators might consider mechanisms by which the certification system could be dismantled by a vote of the participating institutions if it were seen not to serve the common good.

Yet another avenue would be to provide multiple ways for teachers to fulfill the standards and to give each teacher some flexibility in deciding what aspects of his or her work to present. It should be noted that the K-12 certification is moving away from that flexibility, however, in order to improve communication of standards.

Implications of a Visible Distinction Among Faculty. In research on departmental cultures, Barbara Walvoord is currently asking department members, among other things, what distinctions among their members are visible and important, and what the consequences are of those distinctions. In many departments, colleagues and even students are well aware who is tenured or not, who publishes or not, who gets grants or not. A certification system would create another meat-cleaver distinction—between those who are certified or not. How would such a distinction affect departmental and institutional cultures? As proponents of a certification system, we argue that such distinctions could be a powerful lever for cultural change, but we also acknowledge that the issue is complex.

Another issue arising from certification's visibility is how certification will affect teacher morale. As proponents, we argue that almost any system would be an improvement over the present situation. How can morale be maintained when teachers get few rewards for excellence in the classroom, when good teachers cannot move in today's market, and when the reward systems of higher education devalue teaching in myriad ways? Certification could change all that. Further, certification could add another rung to the career ladder of a profession with relatively few rungs at present. The literature on motivation generally holds that rungs are motivating and that one problem with higher education is that it has only two rungs: achieving tenure (usually associated with promotion to associate professor) and promotion to full professor. Its potential to motivate faculty is one of the strongest arguments for a certification system.

Faculty development is another concern. Proponents argue that the certification process could be managed as a chance for growth. The National Board for Professional Teaching Standards makes a similar claim for the portfolios teachers submit and the two-day process in which teachers come to regional centers not only to be tested but also to engage in discussion and self-examination about their teaching. But even if such experiences were provided at the beginning of a teacher's career and even if they worked for most people, would the expensive faculty development aspects of the project continue to be funded? Proponents argue that the system can build in safeguards and that no one wants a system that judges teachers without helping them to develop—that in fact, the combination of certification and rich faculty development may well be a powerful impetus for the improvement of teaching. We argued in our proposal that good faculty development need not be prohibitively expensive, and we pointed to regional teaching workshops, collaboratively funded and sponsored (such as the Baltimore Area Consortium for Writing Across the Curriculum), as examples. But again, the issue remains: how can teachers ensure that the certification system remains developmental in the best sense?

Conclusion

We have elsewhere argued for the establishment of a certification system. In this essay, we have tried to step back and explore the issues inherent in the certification paradigm itself. Each of the six factors that constitute the certification paradigm raises thorny issues. But if such issues are discussed, the resulting national conversation may enrich everyone's thinking about teaching and learning, about the various paradigms for rewarding teaching, about the means of measuring teaching and its outcomes, and about the issue with which this essay began: how can a national market for teaching excellence be created?

References

Bergquist, W. *The Four Cultures of the Academy: Insights and Strategies for Improving Leadership in Collegiate Organizations.* San Francisco: Jossey-Bass, 1992

Chickering, A. W., and Gamson, Z. F. "Seven Principles for Good Practice in Undergraduate Education." *AAHE Bulletin*, March 1987, 3–7.

Kurfiss, J. *Critical Thinking.* Washington, D.C.:American Association of Higher Education, 1987.

Smith, H., and Walvoord, B. "Certifying Teaching Excellence: An Alternative Paradigm to the Teaching Award." *AAHE Bulletin*, 1993, 46 (2), 3–5.

HOKE SMITH is president of Towson State University in Maryland and has also served as chair of the American Association for State Colleges and Universities and of the American Council on Education.

BARBARA WALVOORD is professor of English at the University of Cincinnati.

An old way of honoring teaching lies in the fellowship found within a group of individuals who share an appreciation for excellent teaching; this academy paradigm is becoming more prevalent in institutions today.

Teaching Academies: Honoring and Promoting Teaching Through a Community of Expertise

Nancy Van Note Chism, Jane M. Fraser, Robert L. Arnold

While teaching awards and recognition have long been regular features of most institutional reward systems, only recently have several campuses tried to extend the impact of this reward and recognition through engaging faculty as members of teaching academies. The notion of an academy transforms the concept of singling out individuals into the concept of a community of expertise, changing one-time recognition into an opportunity for continued celebration of excellence.

A *teaching academy* can be loosely defined as a group of faculty who are considered excellent or highly interested in teaching and who have been tapped by their institutions to engage in advocacy, service, or advising on teaching matters. The central idea of the academy is that effective teachers, working through an honorary and service-oriented collective, can have a significant impact on an institution's pursuit of teaching excellence.

A number of teaching academies have sprung up in recent years. The structure, membership, goals, and activities of each academy vary somewhat from institution to institution. An informal survey of known academies was conducted by the authors to describe this variation. The information they obtained has been summarized in a table, which gives brief descriptions of ten of these eleven academies. The chapter then continues with a fuller portrait of one academy, the Academy of Teaching at The Ohio State University, and an analysis of the advantages and disadvantages of teaching academies.

NEW DIRECTIONS FOR TEACHING AND LEARNING, no. 65, Spring 1996 © Jossey-Bass Publishers

Variety Across Academies

Academies can vary in many ways. This section looks at four broad categories: manner of choosing members, affiliation and structure, funding, and goals and activities.

Membership. Although most teaching academies draw their membership from winners of various teaching awards at their institutions, some choose members through a nomination process specifically designed for the academy. In all cases, members are chosen on the basis of demonstrated interest and expertise in teaching. The nomination processes, whether for direct nomination or nomination of teaching award winners, are rigorous and require several kinds of supportive information to be provided to screening committees composed of faculty, students, administrators, and sometimes alumni. In addition to reading supportive letters, many nomination processes make random calls to past students and look for evidence of exemplary evaluations of teaching, involvement in teaching-improvement initiatives, a record of mentoring of new teachers and teaching assistants, and a variety of other documentation. Teachers chosen often receive cash awards, and some receive increments in their base salaries. In a few of the academies, members receive release time for the performance of academy member responsibilities.

The number of members in existing teaching academies varies widely. Some academies may elect as few as one new member each year while one academy elects thirty faculty each year. Some academies have different categories of membership, such as active and emeritus. At Northern Illinois University, for example, members are called Presidential Teaching Professors during their four-year active terms, then become Distinguished Teaching Professors following those terms. Total composition of the academies ranges from about ten to over one hundred members.

Terms of academy members also differ from one institution to another and are tied to academy goals. At San Jose State University, for example, academy members serve one year in a very active role then become alumni members. At a few institutions, members serve limited but renewable terms (for three years, for example, in the case of faculty at University of Wisconsin, Madison). Most other academies induct members for the life of their employment at the institution.

Organizational Affiliation and Structure. Several academies are affiliated with the teaching or faculty development centers at their institutions, and academy members function in either consultant or advisory roles or both. Other academies have relationships with their institutions' academic affairs units. In this arrangement, the academy resembles a special standing committee and is not formally attached to any organizational unit. Of the academies surveyed, only one (at the University of Wisconsin) is affiliated with the faculty senate.

About half of the academies surveyed have an executive committee, and the rest are more informally organized. Only one has a paid staff coordinator not attached to a teaching center. In several of the academies affiliated with teaching centers, the director of the center, sometimes also an academy member, serves as coordinator.

Budget. In keeping with their informal organizational affiliation and structure, most academies have no formal budget line. Those affiliated with teaching centers or academic affairs offices obtain funding through these units as needed and agreed upon for specific purposes. Some academies without operating budgets view the financial awards, project funds, and occasional release time granted to members as the budget. Frequently, award winners are expected to contribute service or to engage in teaching-development projects as part of their award. One academy with a formal budget is the University of Arkansas Teaching Academy, which has a sizable annual operating budget, made possible through an endowment.

Goals and Activities. A common goal among the academies is their interest in fostering teaching excellence at their institutions. They enumerate several related goals.

To advocate the importance of teaching
To create an appropriate reward structure for teaching
To promote a sense of community among teachers
To serve as role models
To foster research on college teaching and learning
To advise the institution on teaching policies and practices

Although their ranges of goals are similar, academies approach the accomplishment of these goals with some striking differences in level of engagement and kind of activities. While some report that they meet only twice per year and are largely advisory, members of the Teaching Scholars Program at San Jose State University meet for two hours per week during the year of their tenure. They and alumni academy members attend a two-day teaching retreat each year and perform an extensive array of teaching-support functions throughout the year.

In addition to engaging in similar activities, academy members at other institutions are involved in task forces to develop systems for documenting and rewarding teaching at their institutions. Members of a few teaching academies serve as representatives of their institutions' teachers to external groups, such as legislative committees, prospective students, professional organizations, and peers at other institutions.

Academy Profiles

Table 4.1 gives brief descriptions of ten of the eleven academies surveyed, facilitating their comparison. The Ohio State University program is not described in the table because it is presented in more detail in the text that follows.

Table 4.1. Comparison of Teaching Academies Surveyed

Institution and Name	Membership	Organizational Structure	Activities
Boston University Center for Teaching Excellence	2–4 members chosen yearly as Metcalf Prize and Award for Excellence in Teaching winners; members of the center for as long as they are with BU	Part of Center for Teaching Excellence; report to Dean of Liberal Arts and Sciences; center director chairs the group	Mentor new faculty; offer workshops on teaching; hold conversations about teaching
Northern Illinois University Presidential Teaching Professorship Program	3 members chosen yearly as Presidential Teaching Professors; after 4-year term, become Distinguished Teaching Professors	Informal; liaison with Provost's Office	Offer seminars on teaching; represent the university with the public; carry out programs related to teaching
Ohio State University	See body of chapter	See body of chapter	See body of chapter
San Jose State University Teacher Scholars Program	8 faculty chosen each year through nomination; 1 active year, then alumni status as Teacher Scholar	Affiliated with Institute for Teaching and Learning; report to Office of Faculty Affairs; coordinated by assistant director of institute	Attend 2-day teaching retreat each year; meet 2 hours each week during semesters; study teaching; help with annual conference on teaching; observe and are observed in class; conduct workshops; mentor other faculty
Thomas Jefferson University College of Allied Health Sciences Center for Faculty Development Associates Program	Winners of 3 teaching awards in allied health sciences	Affiliated with Center for Faculty Development; center director coordinates activities	Observe other faculty and be observed by others in class

Institution	Membership	Structure	Activities
University of Arkansas Teaching Academy	Winners of either of two awards or nominated and voted on by other members; average of 5 per year; appointed for life	President and five board members; chooses board for Teaching and Faculty Support Center; liaison with Office of the Chancellor	Meet once a month to discuss readings; fund receptions, grants, awards, lectures, and workshops on teaching
University of Nebraska Academy of Distinguished Teachers	10 charter members chosen from teaching award winners and nomination and selection process for academy	Liaison with Senior Vice Chancellor for Academic Affairs	Model effective teaching and advocate for teaching; advise Senior Vice Chancellor on teaching and share expertise outside the campus
University of Wisconsin Teaching Academy	30 fellows each year through nomination and selection process; serve 3-year term renewable once; inactive members retain title of Fellow	Executive committee and task forces; report to University Committee and Faculty Senate; half-time coordinator position is funded	Work on task forces for assessing teaching and learning; encourage providing resources to faculty for teaching; provide opportunities for discussion of teaching
University of Wyoming Teaching Academy	3–4 each year through nomination and selection; total less than 5% of eligible faculty; retain titles while at Wyoming; emeritus category	Associates to Center for Teaching Excellence	Mentor junior faculty; present on teaching; participate in center activities; advise provost and president on teaching matters
Virginia Polytechnic Institute Academy of Teaching Excellence	6 per year chosen through 3 teaching awards programs; retain membership as long as at institute	Executive committee; affiliated with Center for Teaching Excellence in Undergraduate Education (CTEUE), which reports to provost	Meet 3 times per year; consult on evaluation of teaching and peer review; advise honors program and committees on teaching; participate in programs such as University Writing Program and Service Learning Program; developed CTEUE and an orientation program for new teaching assistants

Portrait of an Academy of Teaching

Instituted in 1993, the initial members of The Ohio State University Academy of Teaching were the approximately ninety past recipients of the Alumni Award for Distinguished Teaching who were still faculty members at Ohio State. Each year, ten new members are added and there are currently about one hundred members. Members have been opposed to formalizing the academy as an organizational unit, preferring to keep an informal committee structure with ties to the Office of Academic Affairs and the Office of Faculty and TA Development, a teaching support unit.

The academy meets three times a year and has an electronic mailing list for announcements and discussions. Initial meetings have discussed potential academy activities. The stated mission of the academy is to promote excellence in teaching, but selection of appropriate activities for the academy has been difficult. At Ohio State, the Office of Faculty and TA Development (FTAD) coordinates many teaching support services. The academy was not meant to duplicate or replace that office, and an initial issue was to differentiate what each would do.

In May 1993, therefore, the executive council held focus groups in which the membership discussed appropriate activities for the academy. There was broad support for the Academy to do the following: foster excellence in teaching, promote the importance of teaching, help improve the rewards for teaching, help evaluate teaching, help create good publicity for Ohio State, promote a sense of community among academy members, not add to the members' workloads, and work appropriately with other units at Ohio State.

However, the members of the academy were, and continue to be, extremely diverse in opinions. After initial discussions, they have grown to accept the idea that while the academy will never speak with one voice, member diversity is a great source of strength. Selection of activities has also been difficult because the members are very busy. Many members of the academy are extraordinarily active in administration and in faculty governance.

Current activities of the academy include the following:

Members are invited to attend (in academic dress) the president's freshman convocation each fall.

Members are involved as facilitators at the all-day orientation to teaching for new faculty members and the week-long orientation for new TAs.

As part of the provost's teaching fellowship program, members are mentors for graduate students who have received awards for excellence as TAs.

The academy cosponsors talks by visiting scholars (such as "Scholarship Assessed," an April 1994 talk by Ernest Boyer).

At the suggestion of several members, visitors have been invited to academy meetings, and recent meetings have included open and frank discussions with the provost and with the state senator who chairs the State of Ohio Senate Committee on Education.

The academy and FTAD frequently cosponsor events, such as presentations on active learning and teaching portfolios and a panel of Ohio State departments discussing ways to evaluate teaching.

Most significant university committees include at least one academy member.

Jane Fraser, 1994–1995 chairperson of the executive committee of the academy, sums up her reflections on the first years of the academy by saying, "I think that the creation of the academy lit a fuse, but I do not know what is at the other end of that fuse: a sparkler, pretty but with little impact; a firecracker that makes a lot of noise; or, indeed, dynamite, which may, if used constructively, help us dismantle old structures so we can build new ones."

Conclusion: Advantages and Disadvantages of Teaching Academies

Universities with teaching academies report that the advantages, both to the university and to individual faculty members, far outweigh apparent or potential disadvantages. Certainly from a political standpoint, at a time when universities are roundly attacked for lack of attention to teaching, having an academy of teaching calls attention to universities' concern about teaching and, indeed, focuses their attention on the quality of teaching. Such academies may be viewed with some cynicism by faculty because on the surface they appear to be political ploys that exploit teachers' good work. Existing academies have found that this cynicism quickly diminishes, however, when faculty realize the influence that such academies can have on policy within the university. Experience has found that the teaching academy can and does become a force for good teaching that has potential to influence all levels of university activity. The academy creates a community of those who take pride in teaching and of those who excel at teaching. This community can, and does, have greater impact upon policy than the impact of individuals operating in isolation.

Likewise, through members' interaction on the common grounds of teaching, the teaching academy becomes a community, offering opportunities for interdisciplinary contact and activity that go well beyond the confines of individual departments and promote a cross-disciplinary sharing of ideas and techniques relevant to effective and innovative teaching. Important lessons about teaching can be learned from examining ideas about teaching in diverse disciplines; for example, the notion of studio activity in the arts is becoming increasingly important in defining the potential future of teaching in a number of disciplines as we move into an era of technological instruction featuring computer-driven multimedia. Likewise, methods employed in the sciences are adaptable to a number of disciplines throughout the university. The academy provides a convenient forum for the discussion of such ideas.

Academies, by highlighting superior teaching and honoring the most committed teachers, provide teaching models for other faculty within the university. However, academy members also become an elite group, which some faculty resent. Whatever the downside of elitism may be—and one would expect, at the very worst, that it is a decline in morale for those outside the elite—it appears not to have been an impediment in the creation of academies. Of course, ensuring that the selection process is open and fair and rests on clear criteria is important in building confidence in an academy.

Perhaps it is the realization that those within the academy suddenly have a great deal more work to do that is clearly the major disadvantage to academy members; they suddenly find that they are in greater demand. Now identified as spokespeople for an organization committed to high-quality teaching, academy members are often called upon to serve on various university committees, are often expected to participate in ceremonies involving students and parents, and in general, find that demands upon their time have increased. Since, as the very nature of their accomplishments requires, they are already busy people, these additional commitments become problematic. Several universities solve the problem by giving some academy members release time from teaching to pursue the additional commitments, but this action creates a paradox. As it relieves outstanding teachers from teaching duties so they can become spokespeople for outstanding teaching, it also removes the most effective teachers (who incidentally love to teach and find it vastly rewarding) from contact with students. Relieving them from research responsibilities (and many of these individuals are highly productive researchers), simply reinforces the bias that the best teachers are not involved in research. Perhaps the best solution is for university administrators to be sensitive to demands on academy members' time and to relieve them from committee responsibilities not focused on teaching. But even this is difficult because academy members tend to have broad interests that involve them in many aspects of the academy. Every group has both members who are highly visible and willing to assume leadership positions and members who are reserved and participate less. This difference always causes concern within the group but rarely diminishes group effectiveness. Teaching academies are no different, and despite the variance in member activity and the mild discontent of some faculty at being overly busy, academies are an effective—indeed powerful—organizational device for the improvement of teaching.

NANCY VAN NOTE CHISM is director of faculty and TA development at Ohio State University.

JANE M. FRASER is associate professor of industrial, welding and systems engineering and director of the executive committee of the Academy of Teaching at Ohio State University.

ROBERT L. ARNOLD is vice provost for academic support services at Ohio State University.

To honor exemplary teachers, we need to ask whether there are
universal qualities of effective teachers that we can agree upon
as a community.

Characteristics of Exemplary Teachers

Joseph Lowman

Any discussion of honoring teaching makes explicit or implicit assumptions about the kinds of exemplary teaching or teachers that are to be honored. In addition, assumptions are also usually made about whether the individual instructors or the teaching process is to be emphasized most. This chapter focuses explicitly on research about which instructors we would deem exemplary. I have chosen this emphasis not because students or the teaching process are unimportant to what students learn, but because focusing on the characteristics of exemplary instructors offers a place for us to begin to understand the complex human interactions that constitute teaching and learning of the highest order.

The notion of the exemplary college teacher shares much with any idealized concept, such as truth or beauty: it is difficult to achieve consensus on a general definition, but most people think they know a specific example when they see it. The vision of exemplary instructors I present here, then, begins with specific examples before moving on to discuss systematic research about the instructors' general characteristics.

Personal Memories of Exemplary College Teachers

Every educated person can remember two or three particularly outstanding teachers, whether at the secondary, undergraduate, or graduate levels. An informal sampling of these memories shows they are remarkably similar across individuals. For example, when I ask faculty groups to describe outstanding instructors from their pasts they quickly generate a list of ten to fifteen descriptors that is highly similar from group to group. Words such as "stimulating," "dynamic," "enthusiastic," "caring," "motivating," and "knowledgeable" are proposed first, followed by elaborations on images of individuals who are both engaging and capable of motivating and supporting student learning. Informal sampling and anecdotal evidence is, of course, less persuasive than systematic student evaluations of classroom teachers. Fortunately, formal assessments reveal a strikingly similar pattern of characteristics associated with exemplary teaching.

Systematic Assessment of Student Memories

Students have been asked to complete questionnaires about their college teachers for at least three-quarters of this century (Reemers and Brandenburg, 1927), although the use of these forms did not become the norm until the last twenty-five years or so (Seldin, 1984). Feldman's chapter in this volume attests to the increasing use of student evaluations.

What does systematic study of these evaluations tell us about the characteristics of exemplary teachers? In general, factor analysis of Likert scales tells us that most of the variation in the individual questions comes from four underlying dimensions: how (1) clear and (2) interesting were the instructor's classes and how (3) positive and (4) motivating they were in dealings with students (Lowman, 1995). Research continues to explore technical issues in measuring the theoretical structure underlying student ratings (see Chapter Six in this volume, as well as Abrami, d'Apollonia, and Cohen, 1990; Feldman, 1989; Marsh, 1991; Sidanius and Crane, 1989) but on the whole, these four dimensions continue to be identified in statistical analyses of student questionnaires. Because the factors dealing with clarity and interest are almost always stronger than factors dealing with interpersonal relationships, we can conclude that college students put relatively more weight on an instructor's presentation skills, although they would prefer that the individual also be effective interpersonally.

Observational Study of Exemplary Instructors

In 1984, I first published the results of an observational study of over thirty exemplary college professors whom I had identified by simply asking students, faculty, or administrators at several selective Southeastern and New England colleges or universities to identify the notable classroom instructors on their campuses (Lowman, 1995). The same three or four names would emerge after only a few inquiries at a given school, suggesting that there was uniformity of agreement on these instructors' reputations. After interviewing each of these men and women and observing their classes, I formulated a theoretical model of effective college teachers, organizing my observations in a way that is consistent with factor-analytic studies.

Within this perspective, exemplary college teachers were those who excelled on at least one of two dimensions: the ability to generate intellectual excitement in students and/or to generate interpersonal rapport in students. Instructors able to generate the first dimension, *intellectual excitement,* had a solid command of the classroom as a dramatic arena: their abilities to speak energetically and to use gesture and movement before student groups made them highly engaging speakers. Instructors high on this dimension also demonstrated high creativity and an integrative intellectual perspective when they presented content or designed assignments. The net effect of teachers high on this dimension was that students found their classes highly interesting and intellectually stimulating.

The second dimension proposed in this initial model of effective teachers, *interpersonal rapport,* dealt with students and instructors' interactions as people. Teachers who were high on this dimension demonstrated—verbally and nonverbally—strong positive attitudes toward students as people. Whether they learned and used students' names; encouraged interaction before, during, after, or out of class; or simply seemed to be generally warm and positive individuals, these instructors communicated that they liked undergraduates as people. A second characteristic of instructors judged high on the interpersonal rapport dimension was their tendency to use democratic rather than autocratic methods of controlling students. Assignments were made in ways that emphasized students' desire to learn and complete work enthusiastically rather than the instructors' ability to punish them for not doing so. Assignments were also given in ways that, whenever possible, offered students choices about how to meet expectations. My initial model of effective instructors used the term interpersonal rapport to refer to both positive attitudes about students as people and the ability to motivate them from within. Subsequent empirical research, however, indicates that this dimension needs to be broken down into behaviors that communicate interpersonal concern and those that skillfully motivate students.

All of the exemplary instructors I studied were not equally accomplished at the two dimensions: some demonstrated highly developed presentation skills, and others showed an amazing sensitivity to the interpersonal or motivational side of college teaching. Each of the exemplary individuals I studied was at least moderately successful at the skills needed for each of the two dimensions; only one or two were exceptionally skilled at both. Thus, my initial observational study suggested that exemplary college teachers are exceptionally skilled in at least one of two dimensions of college teaching and at least moderately competent in each of them.

Descriptions in Nominations for Teaching Awards

While serving on the Chancellor's Teaching Awards Committee at the University of North Carolina (UNC), Chapel Hill, in 1990, I noted the frequency with which many of the descriptors that appeared in nomination letters from students and faculty fit the two dimensions I had used previously to describe exemplary instructors. Descriptors referring to both presentation and interpersonal skills were abundant. I was fortunate enough to be allowed to make copies and analyze three successive years of nominations—those for 1989, 1990, and 1991— to see to what extent they supported my two-dimensional model.

A data set of over 500 nomination letters was assembled and then coded by research assistants unfamiliar with my teaching model to identify the unique descriptors used in each letter. A list of over 340 words or phrases was constructed and then shortened by combining similar forms of the same concept (for example, "enthusiasm" was combined with "enthusiastic"). A final list of thirty-nine unique descriptors that each occurred at least ten times was identified. The arbitrary criterion of ten appearances was selected to arrive at a workable list of adjectives I could be confident were common in student and faculty perceptions of teachers who deserved to be recognized. Table 5.1 presents these thirty-nine descriptors and the frequency with which each appeared, organized according to the four dimensions in my expanded model of effective college teaching. (See Lowman, 1994, for a more detailed description of this study.)

As can be seen, the data support the importance of both the presentation and interpersonal dimensions in exemplary college teachers. All but six of the thirty-nine descriptors fit easily into the two dimensions of my first teaching model. The interpersonal rapport dimension fits the data better when broken down further into interpersonal concern and motivational skill dimensions, however. The appearance of "dedicated" and "committed" as descriptors indicated that an instructor's perceived investment in teaching is a fourth dimension of what constitutes an exemplary teacher, one that was not included in my 1984 model. Finally, the research on student ratings mentioned earlier, suggesting that the intellectual dimension is slightly more important than the interpersonal, is also supported here. For example, the intellectual excitement dimension contained the single most common descriptor ("enthusiasm") and also the largest number of total appearances of descriptors (398 versus 351 for the two interpersonal rapport categories combined). Still, these differences are slight and should not be overemphasized: students obviously prefer instructors who excel in both kinds of teaching skills.

Exemplary teachers, then, appear to their students to be enthusiastic and engaging speakers who share many of the communication skills used effectively in many group settings. The descriptors gleaned from the teaching nomination forms are remarkably similar to those faculty remembered informally and those culled from factor analytic studies of student rating forms. But surely those nominated for teaching awards are atypical of all faculty because often only the most confident instructors agree to be evaluated by students. Would this portrait remain as sharply drawn if college teachers across a wide range of effectiveness were studied?

Comparisons with Average and Poor Instructors

Herbert Marsh (1986) describes a method of collecting student ratings of teaching that avoids the problems of selective faculty participation in evaluation studies and of the statistical interdependence of student ratings, that is, the fact that many students in a class are rating the same faculty member. Using

Table 5.1. Descriptors Associated with the Enhanced Two-Dimensional Model of Effective College Teaching

Dimension 1: Intellectual Excitement

Adjective	Number of Appearances	Adjective	Number of Appearances
Enthusiastic	68	Engaging	18
Knowledgeable	45	Prepared	16
Inspiring	43	Energetic	15
Humorous	34	Fun	13
Interesting	31	Stimulating	13
Clear	25	Creative	12
Organized	22	Lectures well	11
Exciting	22	Communicator	10
		Total appearances = 398	

Dimension 2A: Interpersonal Concern

Adjective	Number of Appearances	Adjective	Number of Appearances
Concerned	45	Approachable	12
Caring	33	Interested	12
Available	27	Respectful	11
Friendly	18	Understanding	11
Accessible	17	Personable	10
		Total appearances = 196	

Dimension 2B: Effective Motivation

Adjective	Number of Appearances	Adjective	Number of Appearances
Helpful	41	Demanding	14
Encouraging	29	Patient	13
Challenging	28	Motivating	11
Fair	19		
		Total appearances = 155	

Commitment to Teaching

Adjective	Number of Appearances
Dedicated	35
Committed	19
	Total appearances = 54

General Positive Descriptors

Adjective	Number of Appearances
Effective	17
Excellent	17
Outstanding	14
Great	10
	Total appearances = 58

Source: Adapted from Lowman, 1995, p. 32.

his method, one randomly selects students on campus and asks them to rate "the best" and "the worst" teachers they have ever had. This procedure allows data to be collected at any time of the semester without enlisting the cooperation of faculty and ensures that teachers across a wide range of effectiveness are being evaluated.

In the spring of 1993, I used Marsh's method to validate the expanded model of effective teaching (Lowman, 1994). To recruit sophomores, juniors, and seniors to complete teacher evaluation forms, research assistants gathered in a central area of the UNC campus and held a sign that said, "Evaluate Your Teachers, Win a Free Pizza." A group of 198 students who participated in the study produced usable ratings. They were asked to evaluate three specific instructors they had had at UNC: "a very good," "an average," and "a very poor" teacher. Two different rating forms were used, each of which was based on the four dimensions included in the expanded teaching model described above. One form asked students to compete an alphabetized checklist of the thirty-nine adjectives produced in the study of award nominations. Students were instructed to "mark any of the adjectives that apply to your instructor." The second form consisted of ten Likert scale ratings based on the dimensions in the expanded model. Only data from the checklist form are described here.

Table 5.2 presents the average total number of descriptors checked for the "very poor," "average," and "very good" instructors. As is obvious from the displayed means, students gave the three target instructors very different ratings. The total number of descriptors checked for the very poor, average, and very good instructors were 3.6, 12.4, and 25.9, respectively. The same pattern is seen for each of the four dimensions. Not surprisingly, given the low degree of overlap in the ratings for the three groups, a repeated measures multivariate analysis of variance (MANOVA) showed that the total number of adjectives and each of the specific dimensions significantly discriminated the groups (univariate p values in each case were beyond .0001). Thus, the exemplary teachers students selected to rate in this study were quite different on each of the dimensions identified in previous research from instructors the students saw as less effective.

Conclusion

Exemplary college teachers, then, appear to be those who are highly proficient in either one of two fundamental sets of skills: the ability to offer presentations in clearly organized and interesting ways or to relate to students in ways that communicate positive regard and motivate them to work hard to meet academic challenges. All are probably at least completely competent in both sets of skills but outstanding in one or, occasionally, even both of them.

An appropriate way to conclude this chapter is to ask the important question, What impact do these qualities of exemplary teachers have on what students learn? I have previously attempted to answer this question (Lowman, 1995). The model I arrived at delineates three large groups of influences on

**Table 5.2. Average Number of Descriptors
Checked for Different Target Teachers**

| Descriptor Dimensions[a] | Target Teachers | | |
	Very Poor	Average	Very Good
Intellectual excitement (16)	1.5	5.2	10.8
Interpersonal concern (10)	.8	3.6	6.3
Effective motivation (7)	1.0	2.3	4.4
Commitment to teaching (2)	.2	.7	1.6
General positive descriptors (4)	.03	.5	2.6
Total descriptors (39)	3.53	12.3	25.7

Note: Repeated measures MANOVAs showed these means were extremely significantly different ($p <$ .0001) for *each* of the six groups of descriptors.

[a]Numbers following each dimension are the total that could have been checked.

Source: Adapted from Lowman, 1995.

what students learn in any college class and proposes different strengths for their relative direct contributions. What students learn is most influenced by two student qualities: the amount of academic ability students have and how motivated they are to use that ability in a given class. In any class, students who have more aptitude and who work harder will learn more. Next in power of influence is the teacher's contribution, which is a joint product of the amount of teaching ability the teacher has and how motivated that teacher is to apply his or her energies to doing the best possible job in a given course. Finally, the way a course is organized plays a tertiary role in influencing how much students learn. Organizing a course to meet a specific set of objectives (problem-solving or communication skills as opposed to content mastery, for example) will make some difference in what students eventually learn. Similarly, enriching a course with computers or using cooperative teaching techniques is likely to influence what students learn (Johnson and Johnson, 1994; Boettcher, 1992). But the relative direct contribution of course characteristics will always be smaller than that produced by qualities of the teacher and the students. Direct influence on what students learn, then, comes from three sources, only one of which is the teacher.

Fortunately, all college teachers and especially exemplary teachers, have a strong indirect power to promote learning. It results from their ability to influence student motivation, a very powerful direct source of influence. Whether by making their courses clear and engaging or by being positive and supportive of student efforts, exemplary teachers showing the characteristics delineated here make it much more likely that each and every student will be motivated to achieve to his or her maximum ability in a given course.

Being an exemplary presenter and motivator of students, then, is not superfluous. Exemplary teachers are those who are likely to promote unusually high levels of learning in their students, while also creating the positive memories of learning that come to our minds years later in moments of reflection.

References

Abrami, P. C., d'Apollonia, S., and Cohen. P. A. "Validity of Student Ratings of Instruction: What We Know and What We Do Not." *Journal of Educational Psychology,* 1990, *82,* 219–231.

Boettcher, J. V. *101 Success Stories of Information Technology in Higher Education.* Hightstown, N.J.: McGraw-Hill/Primus, 1992.

Feldman, K. A. "The Association Between Student Ratings on Specific Instructional Dimensions and Student Achievement: Refining and Extending the Synthesis of Data from Multisection Validity Studies." *Research in Higher Education,* 1989, *30,* 137–104.

Johnson, D. W., and Johnson, R. T. *Learning Together and Alone: Cooperative, Competitive, and Individualistic Learning.* (4th ed.) Needham Heights, Mass.: Allyn & Bacon, 1994.

Lowman, J. "Professors as Performers and Motivators." *College Teaching,* 1994, *42,* 137–141.

Lowman, J. *Mastering the Techniques of Teaching.* (2nd ed.) San Francisco: Jossey-Bass, 1995.

Marsh, H. W. "Applicability Paradigm: Students' Evaluations of Teaching Effectiveness in Different Countries." *Journal of Educational Psychology,* 1986, *78,* 465–473.

Marsh, H. W. "Multidimensional Students' Evaluations of Teaching Effectiveness: A Test of Alternative Higher-Order Structures." *Journal of Educational Psychology,* 1991, *83,* 285–296.

Seldin, P. *Changing Practices in Faculty Evaluation: A Critical Assessment and Recommendations for Improvement.* San Francisco: Jossey-Bass, 1984.

Sidanius, J., and Crane, M. "Job Evaluation and Gender: The Case of University Faculty." *Journal of Applied and Social Psychology,* 1989, *19,* 174–197.

Reemers, H. H., and Brandenburg, G. C. "Experimental Data on the Purdue Rating Scales for Instructors." *Educational Administration and Supervision,* 1927, *13,* 519–527.

JOSEPH LOWMAN is professor of psychology and assistant dean of arts and sciences at the University of North Carolina, Chapel Hill and the 1995 recipient of the Bowman and Gordon Gray Professorship, UNC's highest teaching award.

A review of the data on the effectiveness of student evaluations reveals that they are a widely used but greatly misunderstood source of information for exemplary teaching.

Identifying Exemplary Teaching: Using Data from Course and Teacher Evaluations

Kenneth A. Feldman

Many colleges and universities are currently putting increased emphasis on good teaching and on designating, honoring, and rewarding good teachers. Consequently, student ratings, long a staple for student course selection, instructor feedback, and administrative personnel decisions, are likely to be applied to this additional purpose. Yet, for all their use, student ratings of instructors and instruction are hardly universally accepted. Some college teachers believe ratings are not reliable, valid, or useful and may even be harmful. Others believe more or less the opposite.

If the credibility of teacher and course evaluations is to be based on more than mere opinion, we must consult the research on their use. In one of the best overviews of this research, after one hundred pages or so of careful, critical, and reflective analysis, Marsh (1987) concludes the following :

> Research described in this article demonstrates that student ratings are clearly multidimensional, quite reliable, reasonably valid, relatively uncontaminated by

Note: This chapter is a much shortened version of a paper commissioned by the National Center on Postsecondary Teaching, Learning, and Assessment for presentation at the second AAHE Conference on Faculty Roles and Rewards, held in 1994. I would like to thank Robert Menges and Maryellen Weimer for their thoughtful suggestions for the original paper and Marilla Svinicki for her invaluable help in condensing it for the present volume. An expanded version, offering fuller analysis and greater detail, can be found under the title, "Identifying Exemplary Teachers and Teaching: Evidence from Student Ratings," in R. P. Perry and J. C. Smart (eds.), *Effective Teaching in Higher Education: Research and Practice* (New York: Agathon Press, 1996, in press).

many variables often seen as sources of potential bias, and are seen to be useful by students, faculty, and administrators. However, the same findings also demonstrate that student ratings may have some halo effect, have at least some unreliability, have only modest agreement with some criteria of effective teaching, are probably affected by some potential sources of bias and are viewed with some skepticism by faculty as a basis for personnel decisions. It should be noted that this level of uncertainty probably also exists in every area of applied psychology and for all personnel evaluation systems. Nevertheless, the reported results clearly demonstrate that a considerable amount of useful information can be obtained from student ratings; useful for feedback to faculty, useful for personnel decisions, useful to students in the selection of courses, and useful for the study of teaching. Probably students' evaluations of teaching effectiveness are the most thoroughly studied of all forms of personnel evaluation, and one of the best in terms of being supported by empirical research [p. 369].

Marsh's tempered conclusions set the stage for the present comments. This chapter analyzes the differential importance of the individual items that constitute the rating forms used to evaluate teachers and courses and explores various interpretations that can be made of information gathered from students about their teachers.

Identifying Instructional Dimensions Important to Effective Teaching

Evaluation instruments try to capture the multidimensionality of teaching. These instruments, as Marsh and Dunkin (1992) point out, are typically constructed from "a logical analysis of the content of effective teaching and the purposes the ratings are intended to serve, supplemented by reviews of previous research and feedback" (p. 146). Less often used is an empirical approach that emphasizes statistical techniques such as factor analysis or multitrait-multimethod analysis. In my own dimensional analysis, I have recently extended an early set of roughly twenty instructional dimensions of teaching components to include twenty-eight dimensions (see Feldman, 1988, 1989a, 1993).

Relation Between Teaching and Student Learning. Based in part on work by d'Apollonia and Abrami (1987, 1988) and Abrami, Cohen, and d'Apollonia (1988), I extended Cohen's (1980b, 1981, 1987) meta-analysis on the association between student achievement and various instructional dimensions (Feldman, 1989a, 1990). The correlations (from this reanalysis) between specific survey items and student achievement are shown in Table 6.1 and range from +.57 to -.11.

Item ranks are shown in parentheses. All but one (for dimension 22) are positive, and all but three (for 22, 23, and 24) are statistically significant. The highest correlations of +.57 and +.56 are for dimensions 1 ("teacher's preparation and course organization") and 2 ("teacher's clarity and understandableness"). The "teacher's pursuit and/or meeting of course objectives" (dimension

Table 6.1. Importance of Instructional Dimensions Using Two Different Indicators of Importance

Instructional Dimension	(1) Correlation with Student Achievement (Larger = More Important; Rank in Parentheses)	(2) Average Standardized Rank Based on Correlation with Overall Evaluation (Smaller = More Important; Rank in Parentheses)
1. Teacher's preparation; organization of course	.57 (1)	.41 (6)
2. Clarity and understandableness	.56 (2)	.25 (2)
3. Teacher pursued and/or met course objectives	.49 (NA)	NA
4. Perceived outcome or impact of instruction	.46 (3)	.28 (3)
5. Teacher's stimulation of interest in the course and its subject matter	.38 (4)	.20 (1)
6. Teacher motivates students to do their best; high standard of performance required	.38 (NA)	NA
7. Teacher's encouragement of questions and discussion, and openness to opinions of others	.36 (5.5)	.60 (11)
8. Teacher's availability and helpfulness	.36 (5.5)	.74 (16)
9. Teacher's elocutionary skills	.35 (7.5)	.49 (10)
10. Clarity of course objectives and requirements	.35 (7.5)	.45 (7)
11. Teacher's knowledge of the subject	.34 (9)	.48 (9)
12. Teacher's sensitivity to, and concern with, class level and progress	.30 (10)	.40 (5)
13. Teacher's enthusiasm (for subject or for teaching)	.27 (11)	.46 (8)
14. Teacher's fairness; impartiality of evaluation of students; quality of examinations	.26 (12)	.72 (14.5)
15. Teacher's classroom management	.26 (NA)	NA
16. Intellectual challenge and encouragement of independent thought (by the teacher and the course)	.25 (13)	.33 (4)
17. Personality characteristics ("personality") of the teacher	.24 (NA)	NA
18. Teacher's concern and respect for students; friendliness of teacher	.23 (14.5)	.65 (12)
19. Nature, quality, and frequency of feedback from teacher to students	.23 (14.5)	.87 (17)
20. Pleasantness of classroom atmosphere	.23 (NA)	NA
21. Nature and value of course material (including its usefulness and relevance)	.17 (16)	.70 (13)
22. Nature and usefulness of supplementary materials and teaching aids	-.11 (17)	.72 (14.5)
23. Difficulty of the course (and workload) —description	.09 (NA)	NA
24. Difficulty of the course (and workload) —evaluation	.07 (NA)	NA

Note: This table has been constructed using data from Tables 1 and 3 in Feldman, 1989a.

3) and "student-perceived outcome or impact of the course" (dimension 4) are the next most highly correlated with student achievement. Somewhat more moderate-sized correlations were found for the instructional dimensions from 5 through 11. Less strongly associated with student achievement are the dimensions from 12 through 21. Dimensions 22 through 24 are not related to student achievement, and nothing could be concluded about dimensions 25 through 28.

Relation Between Specific Aspects of Teaching and Overall Evaluation. If each student's *overall* evaluation of an instructor is made up of the student's evaluation of *specific aspects* of the teacher and the instruction, weighted by the student's estimation of the *relative importance* of these aspects to good teaching, then the *overall* assessment of teachers would be more highly correlated with characteristics those students consider important to good teaching than with those considered less important (compare Crittenden and Norr, 1973). To establish the differential importance of a dimension of teaching, I computed the correlation of each dimension with the global assessment of teachers. (See Feldman, 1976b, 1988, for limitations to this approach.) For each of the instructional dimensions (see Feldman, 1976b, Table 1 and fn. 5), standardized ranks were averaged across a number of pertinent studies. These averages are given in column 2 of Table 6.1 along with their rank from 1 to 17 in the parentheses.

The two analyses, each determining the importance of instructional dimensions from separate studies, have eighteen dimensions in common. The correlation between the ranks shown in parentheses for the separate studies is +.61. Thus, the instructional dimensions that are most highly associated with student achievement (column 1) also tend to be those that best discriminate among teachers with respect to the overall evaluation they receive from students (column 2). Note, however, some discrepancies, especially for "teacher's availability and helpfulness" (high when correlated with achievement but low when correlated with global evaluations) and for "intellectual challenge and encouragement of independent thought" (low when correlated with achievement but high when correlated with global evaluations).

If, relative to the other dimensions, ranks 1 through 6 are thought of as dimensions of high importance, ranks 7 through 12 of moderate importance, and ranks 13 through 17 of low importance, then the results of the two methods show the following pattern.

Both methods indicate that the teacher's preparation, course organization, teacher clarity and understandableness, teacher's stimulation of students' interest, and student-perceived outcome or impact are of high importance. (Items ranked in the top six in both studies.)

Teacher's elocutionary skill, clarity of course objectives and requirements, teacher's knowledge of subject and enthusiasm are of moderate importance relative to other dimensions. (Items ranked between 7 and 12 on both measures.)

Nature, quality, and frequency of feedback to students; nature and value of course material; and nature and usefulness of supplementary materials and teaching aids were of low importance. (Items ranked 13 or lower on both measures.)

Causal Relationships and Other Considerations. Returning to the meaning of the correlations found between specific dimensions and student achievement (column 1), it is important to recognize that these correlations, by themselves, do not establish causal connections between teacher behavior and student achievement. Rather, as Leventhal (1975) points out, some third variable such as student motivation, ability, or aptitude might independently affect both teacher performance and student learning. Establishment of causal connections would require truer experimental designs and the control of extraneous variables. However, where such precautions were taken (Cohen, 1980b, Feldman, 1989a), results were similar to studies where these variables could not be controlled.

Experimental research on cause-effect relationships has been reviewed (selectively) by Murray (1991) who reports that "classroom teaching behaviors, at least in the *enthusiasm* and *clarity* domains, appear to be causal antecedents (rather than mere correlates) of various instructional outcome measures" (p. 161, emphasis added). This supports the findings reported in Table 6.1.

Enthusiastic and expressive attitudes and behaviors of teachers are highlighted in Murray's analysis. In the correlations in Table 6.1, the instructional dimensions of "teachers' enthusiasm (for subject or for teaching)" and "teacher's elocutionary skills" (assumedly an aspect of enthusiasm and expressiveness) are also associated with achievement but only moderately so compared to some of the other instructional dimensions. Note, however, that Murray writes that "behaviors loading on the Enthusiasm (Expressive) factor share elements of spontaneity and stimulus variation, and thus are perhaps best interpreted as serving to elicit and maintain student attention to material presented in class" (p. 146); and, interestingly enough, as the present discussion has emphasized, the instructional dimension of "teacher's stimulation of interest in the course and its subject matter" has been found to be rather highly correlated with students' achievement (ranked fourth) and highly associated, as well, with global evaluation of instruction relative to the other instructional dimensions (ranked first), thus lending support to Murray's observation. Both Murray's analysis and the present analysis emphasize the importance of teacher clarity for effective instruction.

Underlying Mechanisms and Other Considerations. Whether the associations between student learning and teacher's attitudes, behaviors, and practices are established by correlational or experimental studies, we need to know more about the exact psychological and social psychological mechanisms by which these characteristics influence learning. When a large association between an instructional characteristic and student achievement is found, the tendency is to see the finding as self-explanatory. For example, given the size of the correlation involved, it would seem obvious that a teacher who is clear and understandable naturally facilitates students' achievement; little more needs to be said or explained.

In fact, however, we need to specify exactly how those dimensions that affect achievement do so. Indeed, conceptually and empirically specifying such mechanisms in perhaps the most "obvious" connection of them all—that between student achievement and clarity and understandableness of instructors—has turned out to be particularly complex. Likewise, the mechanisms underlying the correlation between the teacher's organization and student achievement have yet to be specifically and fully determined.

Interpreting Teacher and Course Evaluations to Identify Exemplary Teachers

I now turn to the topic of identifying the exemplary teachers. Here students' *global,* or *overall,* evaluations of their teachers (in addition to the more specific evaluations already discussed) are often used.

It is at this point that certain problems and issues in interpreting student ratings become particularly evident. One way of exploring these problems and issues is to focus on the half-truths, if not outright myths, that have cropped up about student assessment and that are, in part, responsible for the unease felt by some faculty, administrators, and students in using student evaluations to identify exemplary teachers.

Myths about Student Evaluations. Aleamoni (1987) has listed a number of "myths" about student ratings of instructors and instruction. I agree that, at least as far as current research shows, the following are untrue (evidence that research does not support these contentions can be found in the following reviews: Cohen, 1980a; Feldman, 1977, 1978, 1987, 1989a, 1989b; Levinson-Rose and Menges, 1981; L'Hommedieu, Menges, and Brinko, 1988, 1990; Marsh, 1984, 1987; and Marsh and Dunkin, 1992):

Students cannot make consistent judgments about the instructor and instruction because of their immaturity, lack of experience, and capriciousness.
Only colleagues with excellent publication records and expertise are qualified to teach and to evaluate their peers' instruction—good instruction and good research are so closely allied that it is unnecessary to evaluate them separately.
Most student rating schemes are nothing more than a popularity contest, with warm, friendly, humorous instructors emerging as winners every time.
Students are not able to make accurate judgments until they have been away from the course and possibly from the university for several years.
Student ratings are both unreliable and invalid.
The time and day the course is offered affects student ratings.
Student ratings cannot be used meaningfully to improve instruction.

For the most part, Aleamoni (1987) also seems correct in calling the following statement a myth: "Gender of the student and the instructor affects student ratings." Consistent evidence cannot be found that either male or female college students routinely give higher ratings to teachers (Feldman, 1977). As for gender of the teacher, a recent review (Feldman, 1993) showed that a majority of the relevant studies found male and female college teachers not to differ in global ratings. However, across studies, evidence suggests that students may rate same-gendered teachers a little more highly than they do opposite-gendered teachers, although other variables may contribute to this finding.

Half-Truths and the Question of Bias. Although Aleamoni (1987) presents the following statements as candidates for status of myth, in reality there are small associations between certain factors and student ratings, as follows:

The size of the class affects student ratings (*slightly* higher ratings are given to teachers of smaller rather than larger courses; see Feldman, 1984; Marsh, 1987).

The level of the course affects student ratings (*slightly* higher ratings are given to upper-level than lower-level courses; see Feldman, 1978).

The rank of the instructor affects student ratings (*slightly* higher ratings are given to teachers of higher rather than lower academic ranks; see Feldman, 1983; Marsh, 1987).

Whether students take the course as a requirement or an elective affects the ratings (*slightly* higher ratings are given to elective courses; see Feldman, 1978; Marsh, 1987).

Whether students are majors or nonmajors affects their ratings (*slightly* higher ratings are given by students who are majors; see Feldman, 1978; Marsh, 1987).

Even if it can be shown that one or more of these factors actually and directly affect students' ratings, the ratings are not necessarily biased by these factors, as is often inferred when such associations are found (for the conceptualization of "bias" used here, see Marsh, 1987). For example, teachers in large classes may receive slightly lower ratings because they indeed are somewhat less effective in larger classes than they are in smaller classes, not because the ratings are biased by students' expressing their dislike of large classes by rating instructors a little lower than they otherwise would. To put the matter in more general terms, certain course characteristics and situational contexts may indeed affect teaching effectiveness, and student ratings may then accurately reflect differences in teaching effectiveness. However, those making decisions about promotions and teaching awards should consider that it may be somewhat harder to be effective in some courses than others.

The idea that "the grades or marks students receive in the course are highly correlated with their ratings of the course and instructor" (Aleamoni, 1987) is another candidate for the status of myth, since grades are not *highly* correlated with student ratings. However, almost all of the available research does show a small or even modest positive association between grades and evaluation (see Feldman, 1976a, 1977; Stumpf and Freedman, 1979). Research has also shown that some part of the positive correlation has a basis in reality and therefore is unbiased: students who learn more earn higher grades and thus legitimately give higher evaluations.

The academic discipline of a course is yet another correlate of—and therefore, possible influence on—teacher and course evaluations. Reviewing eleven studies, I found that teachers in different academic fields tend to be rated somewhat differently, with teachers in English, humanities, arts, and languages being rated higher than those in the social sciences, followed by those in the natural sciences, mathematics and engineering (Feldman, 1978). More recent data using two national evaluation instruments (IDEA and SIR) reported differences similar to those in my review (Cashin, 1990; Cashin and Clegg, 1987; Cashin and Sixbury, 1993). Among possible causes of these differences are the following: some courses are harder to teach than others; some fields have better teachers than others; and students in different major fields rate differently because of possible differences in their attitudes, academic skills, goals, motivations, learning styles, and perceptions of good teaching. However, Cashin and Sixbury (1993) caution institutions to look carefully at disciplinary differences in evaluations to be sure that they are a function of something other than teaching effectiveness before adjusting the results of students' evaluations in different disciplines.

Conclusion

Nothing I have written here is meant to imply that course and teacher evaluations are the only means of identifying exemplary teachers and teaching. Discussions about teaching portfolios (see, for example, Edgerton, Hutchings, and Quinlan, 1991, and Chapter Nine of this volume) emphasize the importance of diverse information from a variety of sources. Yet, when properly administered and interpreted, the global and specific items contained in student surveys can serve as an important source of information for identifying exemplary teachers and teaching.

References

Abrami, P. C., Cohen, P. A., and d'Apollonia, S. "Implementation Problems in Meta-Analysis." *Review of Educational Research*, 1988, *58*, 151–179.

Aleamoni, L. "Student Rating Myths Versus Research Facts." *Journal of Personnel Evaluation in Education*, 1987, *1*, 111–119.

Cashin, W. E. "Students Do Rate Different Academic Fields Differently." In M. Theall and J. Franklin (eds.), *Student Ratings of Instruction: Issues for Improving Practice*. New Directions for Teaching and Learning, no. 43. San Francisco: Jossey-Bass, 1990.

Cashin, W. E., and Clegg, V. L. "Are Student Ratings of Different Academic Fields Different?" Paper presented at the annual meeting of the American Educational Research Association, Washington, D.C.: April 1987. (ED 286 935)

Cashin, W. E., and Sixbury, G. R. *Comparative Data by Academic Field*. IDEA Technical Report No. 8. Manhattan: Kansas State University, Center for Faculty Evaluation and Development, 1993.

Cohen, P. A. "Effectiveness of Student-Rating Feedback for Improving College Instruction: A Meta-Analysis of Findings." *Research in Higher Education,* 1980a, *13,* 321–341.

Cohen, P. A. "A Meta-Analysis of the Relationship Between Student Ratings of Instruction and Student Achievement." Unpublished doctoral dissertation, University of Michigan, Ann Arbor, 1980b.

Cohen, P. A. "Student Ratings of Instruction and Student Achievement." *Review of Educational Research,* 1981, *51,* 281–309.

Cohen, P. A. "A Critical Analysis and Reanalysis of the Multisection Validity Meta-Analysis." Paper presented at the annual meeting of the American Educational Research Association, Washington, D.C.: April 1987. (ED 283 876)

Crittenden, L. S., and Norr, J. L. "Student Values and Teacher Evaluation: A Problem in Person Perception." *Sociometry,* 1973, *36,* 143–151.

d'Apollonia, S., and Abrami, P. C. "An Empirical Critique of Meta-Analysis: The Literature on Student Ratings of Instruction." Paper presented at the annual meeting of the American Educational Research Association, Washington, D.C.: April 1987.

d'Apollonia, S., and Abrami, P. C. "The Literature on Student Ratings of Instruction: Yet Another Meta-Analysis." Paper presented at the annual meeting of the American Educational Research Association, New Orleans, La., 1988.

Edgerton, R., Hutchings, P., and Quinlan, K. *The Teaching Portfolio: Capturing the Scholarship in Teaching.* Washington, D.C.: American Association for Higher Education, 1991.

Feldman, K. A. "Grades and College Students' Evaluation of Their Courses and Teachers." *Research in Higher Education,* 1976a, *4,* 69–111.

Feldman, K. A. "The Superior College Teacher from the Students' View." *Research in Higher Education,* 1976b, *5,* 243–288.

Feldman, K. A. "Consistency and Variability Among College Students in Rating Their Teachers and Courses: A Review and Analysis." *Research in Higher Education,* 1977, *6,* 223–274.

Feldman, K. A. "Course Characteristics and College Students' Ratings of Their Teachers: What We Know and What We Don't." *Research in Higher Education,* 1978, *9,* 199–242.

Feldman, K. A. "Seniority and Experience of College Teachers as Related to Evaluation They Receive from Students." *Research in Higher Education,* 1983, *18,* 3–124.

Feldman, K. A. "Class Size and College Students' Evaluations of Teachers and Courses: A Closer Look." *Research in Higher Education,* 1984, *21,* 45–116.

Feldman, K. A. "Research Productivity and Scholarly Accomplishment of College Teachers as Related to Their Instructional Effectiveness: A Review and Exploration." *Research in Higher Education,* 1987, *26,* 227–298.

Feldman, K. A. "Effective College Teaching from the Students' and Faculty's View: Matched or Mismatched Priorities?" *Research in Higher Education,* 1988, *28,* 291–344.

Feldman, K. A. "The Association Between Student Ratings of Specific Instructional Dimensions and Student Achievement: Refining and Extending the Synthesis of Data from Multisection Validity Studies." *Research in Higher Education,* 1989a, *30,* 583–645.

Feldman, K. A. "Instructional Effectiveness of College Teachers as Judged by Teachers Themselves, Current and Former Students, Colleagues, Administrators, and External (Neutral) Observers." *Research in Higher Education,* 1989b, *30,* 137–194.

Feldman, K. A. "Afterword to 'The Association Between Student Ratings of Specific Instructional Dimensions and Student Achievement: Refining and Extending the Synthesis of Data from Multisection Validity Studies.'" *Research in Higher Education,* 1990, *31,* 315–318.

Feldman, K. A. "College Students' Views of Male and Female College Teachers. Part II: Evidence from Students' Evaluations of Their Classroom Teachers." *Research in Higher Education,* 1993, *34,* 151–211.

Levinson-Rose, J., and Menges, R. L. "Improving College Teaching: A Critical Review of Research." *Review of Educational Research,* 1981, *51,* 403–434.

Leventhal, L. "Teacher Rating Forms: Critique and Reformulation of Previous Validation Designs." *Canadian Psychological Review,* 1975, *16,* 269–276.

L'Hommedieu, R., Menges, R. J., and Brinko, K. T. "The Effects of Student Ratings Feedback to College Teachers: A Meta-Analysis and Review of Research." Unpublished manuscript, Northwestern University, Center for the Teaching Professions, 1988.

L'Hommedieu, R., Menges, R. J., and Brinko, K. T. "Methodological Explanations for the Modest Effects of Feedback." *Journal of Educational Psychology*, 1990, *82*, 223–241.

McKeachie, W. J. "Instructional Evaluation: Current Issues and Possible Improvements." *Journal of Higher Education*, 1987, *58*, 344–350.

Marsh, H. W. "Students' Evaluations of University Teaching: Dimensionality, Reliability, Validity, Potential Biases, and Utility." *Journal of Educational Psychology*, 1984, *76*, 707–754.

Marsh, H. W. "Students' Evaluations of University Teaching: Research Findings, Methodological Issues, and Directions for Future Research." *International Journal of Educational Research*, 1987, *11*, 253–388.

Marsh, H. W., and Dunkin, M. J. "Students' Evaluations of University Teaching: A Multidimensional Approach." In J. C. Smart (ed.), *Higher Education: Handbook of Theory and Research*, Vol. 8. New York: Agathon Press, 1992.

Murray, H. G. "Effective Teaching Behaviors in the College Classroom." In J. C. Smart (ed.), *Higher Education: Handbook of Theory and Research*, Vol. 8. New York: Agathon Press, 1991.

Perry, R. P. "Perceived Control in College Students: Implications for Instruction in Higher Education." In J. C. Smart (ed.), *Higher Education: Handbook of Theory and Research*, Vol. 7. New York: Agathon Press, 1991.

Stumpf, S. A., and Freedman, R. D. "Expected Grade Covariation with Student Ratings of Instruction: Individual Versus Class Effects." *Journal of Educational Psychology*, 1979, *71*, 293–302.

KENNETH A. FELDMAN *is professor of sociology at the State University of New York, Stony Brook.*

*Are traditional sources of information about exemplary teaching
effective for identifying such teachers?—a review of the research
and a proposal.*

Identifying Exemplary Teachers:
Evidence from Colleagues,
Administrators, and Alumni

John A. Centra

This chapter examines the quality of the evidence that colleagues, administrators, and alumni can provide in identifying exemplary teachers. While student evaluations of teaching are an increasing source of information about instructors, a reliable measurement system demands that we use more than one source of data.

Research on Evaluation by Colleagues, Chairs, and Deans

Colleagues and chairs can provide critical information about teaching effectiveness not available from other sources. Neither students, who lack the background and experience, nor deans, who lack the time and exposure, are able to provide the same perspective on an individual's teaching. *Colleagues,* particularly those from similar disciplines, can best judge content knowledge and other specialized aspects of teaching. *Department chairs* may be considered as colleagues or administrators, depending on whether theirs is a rotating or permanent assignment. Colleagues and chairs typically know more about a given faculty member's performance than do deans.

Evaluations by colleagues, chairs, and deans can use a numerical rating scale (such as a one-to-five scale ranging from poor to excellent) or a ranking of all possible candidates from high to low. Ranking candidates has produced acceptable levels of reliability in the military and other nonacademic settings (Love, 1981; Kane and Lawler, 1978). Reliability in rankings means that an acceptable level of consensus has been reached after receiving rankings from a sufficient number of rankers. Reliability will usually increase as the number of rankers increases.

Colleagues, chairs, and deans may employ various kinds of data for evaluations. Classroom observation, course criteria beyond classroom performance, teaching portfolios, and overall evaluations are considered here.

Classroom Observations. Colleague, chair, and dean evaluations are sometimes equated with classroom observations, but that need not be the case. Research has shown that when colleague ratings are based solely on classroom observations, only slight interrater agreement can be expected. A study of colleague ratings of teaching at an institution in its first year of operation, when teaching reputations had not yet been established, found only slight consensus among three classroom observers (Centra, 1975). Increasing the number of observers or training colleagues in making judgments would probably lead to increased consensus, but both options also require much more faculty time.

Criteria Beyond Classroom Performance. While classroom observations can undoubtedly add a useful dimension to the evaluation of teaching, other criteria are also important. McKeachie and Cohen (1980) identified ten criteria of effective teaching that colleagues (and probably chairs and deans to some extent) are best able to judge: instructor mastery of content, selection of course content, appropriateness of course objectives, appropriateness of course materials, commitment to teaching and student learning, support of departmental instructional efforts, course organization, appropriateness of devices for evaluating student learning, application of appropriate methodology for teaching specific content areas, and student achievement based on student performance on exams and projects (p. 148).

The first six of these ten criteria are best evaluated by colleagues in the same field as the person being evaluated. Other criteria, such as course organization, teaching methods, and evaluation devices can be judged by colleagues who are outside the department but who have some knowledge of good instructional design. Judgments on the criteria can be made by using questionnaires (Centra, 1993), by examining course documents, or by visiting the classroom, though standards of performance in each of these areas are often ill defined.

Teaching Portfolios. The teaching portfolio (see Chapter Nine, also) is another way in which faculty members can document their performance as teachers. Colleagues are the intended reviewers of these portfolios, evaluating them for evidence of course planning and preparation, presentations of teaching, methods for evaluating and giving feedback to students, and keeping up with the profession (Edgerton, Hutchings, and Quinlan, 1991). In each of these domains, a teacher is expected to comment or reflect in the portfolio about what he or she did and why he or she did it. These reflections should include what the teacher was thinking about and hoping for while making instructional decisions. The portfolio should also include a two- to four-page personal statement by the teacher, discussing his or her philosophy, abilities, and skills related to teaching.

I studied the use of the portfolio at one college that examined portfolios in making summative decisions on faculty (Centra, 1994). Two faculty colleagues and one of four deans rated each portfolio. One colleague was selected by the individual faculty member, and the second was selected by the dean. Deans rated only faculty members in their schools. Portfolios included examples of faculty members' teachings and their reflections on their motivational, interpersonal, and intellectual skills as teachers. Each skill was defined in detail, and teachers were to provide examples of how they exhibited the skills in their teaching. Under these circumstances, colleagues selected by the faculty members gave the highest evaluations and tended to differ from other colleagues or the dean on the evaluations of teaching effectiveness. Moreover, the evaluations by these teacher-selected colleagues did not correlate with independently collected student evaluations, whereas the evaluations by the deans and the dean-selected colleagues did. Clearly, *who* rates the portfolios is a critical aspect of their usefulness in summative decisions.

A brief training session makes colleague evaluations of portfolio material more reliable. In a study in which six elected faculty members rated faculty dossiers after first discussing the criteria and examples of high and low ratings, the agreement among colleagues was very high (Root, 1987). Thus, it would appear that an appropriate group of colleagues can make valid and reliable evaluations of teaching effectiveness based on the kind of information included in a teaching portfolio.

Overall Ratings of Teachers. Most studies of colleague and administrator evaluations of teacher effectiveness have analyzed colleagues' and administrators' *overall* evaluations. These overall, or global, evaluations are typically based on unspecified sources of information. No doubt teacher reputations and comments from students play a major role in making judgments. It is not surprising, therefore, that across fourteen studies, the average correlation between colleague and student evaluation of teachers was .55 (Feldman, 1989). In addition to hearing students' informal comments, colleagues may learn about a teacher's effectiveness from published student evaluations. Colleagues also gain impressions of an individual's teaching ability from conversations with one another. In one of the few studies that asked colleagues to identify the basis for their evaluations of beginning teachers, most identified conversations with the new teacher, with students, or with both (Fink, 1984). About half also said they had seen formal student evaluation results.

The fourteen studies that compared student and colleague ratings found no difference in the distribution of ratings of teachers given by colleagues and students. Whatever the basis for the evaluations, the size of the correlation between colleagues and students (.55) indicates that there would be considerable but certainly not total agreement in the lists of effective teachers identified by each group. To a somewhat lesser extent, the same may be said for selections by colleagues in comparison to administrators (mainly department chairs). Their evaluations of teachers had an average correlation of .48 (Feldman, 1989). Administrator ratings of teachers had an average correlation of

.39 with those of students, indicating relatively modest overlap between these two groups. The lowest correlations were for teacher self-ratings compared to administrators' ratings (.08), and self-ratings compared to colleagues' ratings (.15). Not surprisingly, this indicates that self-ratings seem to be of little value in selecting award winners. Therefore self-evaluations in a teaching portfolio or dossier should be interpreted very cautiously.

Colleagues are comparatively more consistent in judging the research productivity of fellow faculty members. Kremer (1990) found that colleagues' evaluations of research were more reliable (that is, exhibited greater agreement among colleagues) than their evaluations of teaching or service. Root (1987), as mentioned earlier, studied six elected faculty members who independently rated teaching, research, and service dossiers of individual faculty members. Together, they reviewed and discussed the criteria before making their ratings, using cases that illustrated high and low ratings.

The reliabilities of the evaluations of this six-member committee (based on average intercorrelations) were very high (above .90) for each of the three performance areas. In fact, Root concluded that a three-member committee could provide sufficiently reliable evaluations. The strongest agreement among raters was in evaluating research. Little correlation, however, was found between ratings of research, teaching, and service, indicating that individuals who were productive in one area were not necessarily productive in the other two.

Evidence from Alumni

Surveys of alumni have indicated that they identify the same characteristics of effective teaching as do current students, faculty members, and administrators. Alumni also appear to rate individual teachers similarly to current students. An early study by Drucker and Remmers (1951) found positive correlations ranged from .40 to .68 on such dimensions of teaching as presentation of the subject matter and attitude toward students. I found a higher correlation, .75, for overall ratings of teachers by current students and alumni who had graduated up to five years earlier (Centra, 1974). Both of these studies had different groups rating the same teachers each time. Overall and Marsh (1980) collected ratings from the *same* students at the end of their courses and at least one year after graduation. For one hundred courses, end-of-course ratings correlated .83 with retrospective overall course ratings. For individual rating items, the correlations were also in the low .80s. These three studies indicate very good stability in student evaluations, although the correlations seem to decrease with passing time, suggesting that students' memories of instructor characteristics fade with time.

Even though the correlations were high, a closer look at some of the ratings indicated noteworthy exceptions. In almost all groups, a given teacher might be named a "best" teacher by some students and a "worst" teacher by others (Centra, 1974). Stability of ratings aside, these findings indicate that many teachers can have a special appeal or lack of appeal for a few students.

As some writers have pointed out, teachers are not simply "good" or "bad"; they are good or bad with particular students (McKeachie, Lin, and Mann, 1971). Most institutions, however, would prefer to give teaching awards to teachers who are effective with a large proportion of students on the grounds that good teachers also attempt to reach as many students in their classes as they can.

Conclusion

Colleagues, administrators, students, and alumni have all identified similar general characteristics of what effective teachers do. Research indicates that colleagues, administrators, and alumni can each make valid evaluations of individual teachers. Although alumni and current student ratings of teachers are often highly correlated, for the purposes of selecting exemplary teaching award winners, the alumni can provide a longer-term view based on postclassroom experiences. Colleague and administrative evaluations are best made when colleagues and administrators are members of committees that have access to documented evidence of teaching. Institutions may want to adopt a two-stage process of identifying teaching award winners. In the first stage, nominators use a form that allows them to rate and describe the characteristics that make their nominees exemplary. In the second stage, teaching portfolios provided by each nominee are used as basis for committee selection of award winners.

While this proposal is not a perfect system, the solicitation of evaluations from a wide range of sources can only increase the richness of the data available to make award decisions. At the same time, the contributors to the process will become more aware of their own values in the area of effective teaching and the quality of the teaching that surrounds them.

References

Centra, J. A. "The Relationship Between Student and Alumni Rating of Teachers." *Educational and Psychological Measurement*, 1974, 34 (2), 321–326.

Centra, J. A. "Colleagues as Raters of Classroom Instruction." *Journal of Higher Education*, 1975, 46, 327–337.

Centra, J. A. "Use of the Teaching Portfolio and Student Evaluations for Summative Evaluation." Paper presented at the American Educational Research Association meeting, Atlanta, Ga., April 1993.

Centra, J. A. "The Use of the Teaching Portfolio and Student Evaluations for Summative Evaluation." *Journal of Higher Education*, 1994, 65, 555–570.

Drucker, A. J., and Remmers, H. H. "Do Alumni and Students Differ in their Attitudes Toward Instructors?" *Journal of Educational Psychology*, 1951, 42 (3), 129–143.

Edgerton, R., Hutchings, P., and Quinlan, K. *The Teaching Portfolio: Capturing the Scholarship in Teaching*. Washington, D.C.: American Association for Higher Education, 1991.

Feldman, K. A. "Instructional Effectiveness of College Teachers as Judged by Teachers Themselves, Current and Former Students, Colleagues, Administrators, and External (Neutral) Observers." *Research in Higher Education*, 1989, 30, 137–194.

Fink, L. D. "The First Year of College Teaching." New Directions for Teaching and Learning, no. 17. San Francisco: Jossey-Bass, 1984.

Kane, J. S., and Lawler, E. E. "Methods of Peer Assessment." *Psychological Bulletin,* 1978, *85,* 555–586.

Kremer, J. "Constant Validity of Multiple Measures in Teaching, Research, and Service and Reliability of Peer Ratings." *Journal of Educational Psychology,* 1990, *82,* 213–218.

Love, K. G. "Comparison of Peer Assessment Methods: Reliability, Validity, Friendship, Bias, and User Reaction." *Journal of Applied Psychology,* 1981, *66,* 451–457.

McKeachie, W. J., and Cohen, P. A. "The Role of Colleagues in the Evaluation of College and University Teaching." *Improving College and University Teaching,* 1980, *28* (4), 147–154.

McKeachie, W. J., Lin, Y., and Mann, W. "Student Ratings of Teacher Effectiveness: Validity Studies." *American Educational Research Journal,* 1971, *8,* 435–445.

Overall, J. U., and Marsh, H. W. "Student's Evaluations of Instruction: A Longitudinal Study of their Stability." *Journal of Educational Psychology,* 1980, *72,* 321–325.

Root, L. S. "Faculty Evaluation: Reliability of Peer Assessments of Research, Teaching, and Service." *Research in Higher Education,* 1987, *26,* 71–84.

JOHN A. CENTRA is professor of higher education at Syracuse University in New York.

Since the ultimate goal of teaching is to facilitate learning, shouldn't the most appropriate measure of effective teaching be its relationship to student learning?

Relating Exemplary Teaching to Student Learning

Thomas A. Angelo

Before we can honor exemplary teaching, we must first identify it. As others in this volume have noted, this prerequisite raises thorny questions. For example, how can we tell when a teacher is doing exemplary work? What constitutes appropriate and acceptable evidence? How can we distinguish satisfactory teaching from exemplary teaching?

This chapter aims to suggest productive ways to think about assessing exemplary teaching and to identify some useful resources to inform next steps. To that end, I advance three main arguments. First, I assert that the most meaningful measure of teaching is student learning, and that we should focus evaluation of college teachers accordingly. Second, I maintain that recent research in psychology, cognitive science, and education—and the best practice in assessment—can provide us with practical guidelines for assessing the effects of teaching on learning. And third, I point out that the technical and practical barriers to assessing teaching's effects on learning can be overcome, if we value learning highly enough to do so.

Underlying Assumptions

Five assumptions inform this chapter. First and foremost, I assume that the purpose of teaching is to help students learn more effectively and efficiently than they would on their own. Compare this to the practice of assessing faculty members' teaching effectiveness only in light of their students' perceptions or, at best, the perceptions of their students and a colleague or two. We should call teaching exemplary only when we have face-valid evidence that it is powerfully, positively affecting student learning. In other words, exemplary teaching is that which demonstrably promotes exemplary learning.

Second, I presume that a sense of professional and ethical responsibility should motivate faculty to assess and document how our teaching affects students' learning and to work systematically to improve our effectiveness. Of course, political and economic pressures virtually ensure that administrators will push for more evaluation and better evidence of teaching effectiveness. Nonetheless, I assume that the primary reason for assessing and evaluating teaching is to promote better teaching and learning. After all, exemplary teaching is only of use if other teachers can learn from the exemplars and improve their own practice.

Third, I believe that we now know enough about effective teaching, learning, and assessment to assess and evaluate college teaching in meaningful, responsible, and productive ways—but that we rarely do so. Fourth, I assume that the primary reasons we fail to use what we know are not technical or methodological but typically personal and political. That is, we fear it would be too much work, too potentially threatening to individual comfort or careers, and too likely to cause conflicts with our colleagues.

Finally, I am convinced that there is no single simple one-size-fits-all method to assess the effects of teaching on learning. Assessing teaching is a highly contextual process, which requires the development of "communities of shared reflective judgment" (Shulman, 1993, p.6) at departmental and institutional levels.

A Note on Terms

I use *assessment* throughout as a broad umbrella term, to mean the systematic collection, analysis, interpretation, and use of information to understand and improve teaching and learning. *Evaluation,* in this context, has a narrower meaning: the use of a subset of the information generated by assessment to make judgments of relative value (Gardiner, 1995, p. 1). Thus, while responsible departments and instructors assess the quality of teaching and learning continuously in many formal and informal ways, they evaluate only when it is necessary to make decisions about grades, graduation, merit raises, promotion, tenure—or awards for exemplary teaching.

In order to identify, assess, evaluate, and honor exemplary teaching, we need to know *what* to look for and *where* to look. Then we need guidelines on *how* to look at and assess it. In the jargon of assessment and evaluation, the criteria of exemplary teaching will tell us *what* to look for; the indicators *where*; and the standards *how*. Say, for example, that a campuswide faculty assessment committee reaches consensus that being well-organized is key to effective teaching. In that case, being well-organized is a *criterion*. *Indicators* related to that criterion might be an instructor's syllabi, directions on assignments, the explicit structure of his or her lectures, and the like. And the *standards* would be the levels of organization the committee agrees to use to discriminate among poor, adequate, and exemplary examples of syllabi, assignments, and lectures.

How Can We Assess the Effects of Teaching on Learning?

The simplest, most direct answer to this question is to assess what students know just before instruction begins and again at the end of instruction. The difference between the pre- and postassessment results—whether positive, neutral, or negative—indicate the effects of teaching on learning, the so-called value added.

While I am convinced we need to do exactly this, I am also keenly aware that pre- and postassessment approach is fraught with problems. The same is true of other evaluations of teaching, of course. There is no single method of assessing teaching or learning that is entirely valid and reliable. This does not mean, however, that assessing the effects of teaching on learning is impossible— or even impractical. It simply means that we need to follow guidelines for good practice in assessment.

Guidelines for Good Practice in Assessment. In two pages, Alexander Astin and other assessment experts offer nine well-supported Principles of Good Practice for Assessing Student Learning. While all nine principles bear on the question at hand, Principle 2 is of particular relevance. It states: "Assessment is most effective when it reflects an understanding of learning as multidimensional, integrated, and revealed in performance over time" (Astin and others, 1992, p.2). In relation to assessing the effects of teaching on learning, this means we need to use multiple methods of assessment, focus on multiple dimensions and indicators of effective teaching and learning, involve multiple assessors in the process, and carry out the assessment over a long enough time to detect learning if and when it occurs. In short, assessment plans that depend only on end-of-term student evaluations, a single classroom visit by the department chair, or pre- and posttest scores are examples of poor assessment practice.

Using Multiple Methods. The pre-postassessment approach attempts to get a fairly direct measure of teaching's effects on learning. Other direct measures include using the results of standardized tests, such as national licensing exams, Graduate Record Exams, or other professional examinations. Alternatively, the external evaluator approach, which has come back into fashion in response to assessment mandates, has a long history in areas such as honors programs.

In education, however, we have to depend in large part on indirect measures. But which indirect indicators of learning should we assess and, if possible, measure? Recent research in psychology, cognitive science, and education has demonstrated that certain conditions, practices, and processes are more highly correlated with learning than others. So, by looking for and assessing indicators that are strongly correlated with effective learning, we can improve our assessment and evaluation of teaching. At the same time, we can satisfy the second criterion of good assessment: the need to assess multiple dimensions and indicators.

Assessing Multiple Dimensions. While it is true that no one can "learn" anyone else anything, it is also true that teachers play central roles in promoting student learning. Research on learning suggests several criteria and indicators of exemplary teaching.

The monumental analytical summary of twenty years of higher education research done by Pascarella and Terenzini (1991) identified several variables affecting the quantity and quality of learning in college. The number one explanatory variable is the quantity and quality of student academic effort. Number two is usually students' interactions with other students about their academic work. I write "usually" because in settings where students have little or no access to other students, their interactions with faculty can easily become the second most powerful influence on learning. So the third—or sometimes second—most important variable is students' interactions with teachers about their academic work. Teacher-student interaction that involve learning can take place in the lecture hall, the laboratory, the professor's office, or via e-mail.

These three variables, and other important ones, crop up repeatedly in research-based guidelines for effective teaching and learning practice (for example, Svinicki, 1991; McKeachie and others, 1994; McKeachie, Pintrich, Lin, and Smith, 1986; Angelo, 1993). The most widely known and applied are the Seven Principles for Good Practice in Undergraduate Education, which state that good practice: (1) encourages student-faculty contact, (2) encourages cooperation among students, (3) encourages active learning, (4) gives prompt feedback, (5) emphasizes time on task, (6) communicates high expectations, and (7) respects diverse talents and ways of learning (Chickering and Gamson, 1991; Sorcinelli, 1991, contains a useful review of the research supporting these seven principles).

Thanks to meta-analytic work by Kenneth Feldman (1988; see also Chapter Six), we know that faculty and students are working from the same basic checklist when they evaluate teaching. Feldman finds nine key characteristics or criteria that students and teachers rate as most important: knowledge of the subject or discipline, course preparation and organization, clarity and understandability, enthusiasm for subject/teaching, sensitivity to/concern with students' level and learning progress, availability and helpfulness, quality of examinations, impartiality in evaluating students, and overall fairness to students.

Students and teachers differ in the relative importance they assign to various criteria. For example, students tend to value enthusiasm more than faculty do; faculty tend to give content knowledge higher priority than students do. Broad agreement exists in our academic culture about the most important characteristics of good teachers and good teaching.

Not surprisingly perhaps, it turns out that many of the characteristics just mentioned correlate positively with effective learning. We know, for example, that students tend to be more motivated to learn when they perceive their teachers as enthusiastic, well prepared, clear, fair, and interested in them. And on average, well-motivated students learn more than poorly motivated ones. So, along with the Seven Principles, we have another practical, empirically derived list of criteria with which to focus teaching assessment and evaluation.

The implications for assessment are manifold. For example, faculty within a department or institution can develop specific local criteria, standards, and indicators for assessing teaching based on some or all of these general principles. And the path has already been cleared. Chickering, Gamson, and Barsi have developed prototype inventories for faculty and institutions based on the seven principles (Chickering and Gamson, 1991, pp. 71–100), and Barsi (1991) provides illustrative vignettes on the use of these inventories. The big point here is not that one should adopt a particular list of principles or a specific inventory of practices, but rather that there *are* empirically based principles and practices that are correlated with student learning which can, in turn, inform our assessment of teaching.

Taking any one of these collections or cross-referencing them all, we could list several dimensions that would hold promise for identifying exemplary teaching. While failure on any one dimension would not necessarily indicate poor teaching, consistently high performance across a majority of these dimensions would certainly mark exemplary teaching in anyone's view.

Using Multiple Assessors. As we have seen, good practice in assessment requires a focus on multiple indicators, using multiple measures, over time. But it also requires multiple sources of data and the differing perspectives of multiple assessors to be credible and useful. In assessing teaching, it is important to remind ourselves that we have several possible sources of data and perspectives to draw on. As Kahn (1993, pp. 115–116) notes: "Too often, 'teaching evaluation' is equated with 'student evaluation.' While student evaluations are essential to assessing teaching, they do not give us a full picture of teaching effectiveness and should always be used in combination with information from other sources." Experts on faculty assessment and evaluation agree that we need teaching assessment data from at least three different sources: from the instructors themselves, their students, and their faculty peers and colleagues (Cashin, 1989; Centra, 1993; Braskamp and Ory, 1994).

Qualities best assessed by the teacher. Teachers know better than anyone else what they value and intend. Thus, from the instructor, we need information on goals, objectives, and plans. We need to know, in more detail than most syllabi probably reveal, what the teacher is trying to accomplish. What kinds of learning is the course designed to promote? Is it primarily focused on teaching students facts and principles of a discipline, developing discipline-related skills, enhancing broader critical thinking and problem-solving skills, or deepening appreciations? How, specifically, does the instructor plan to promote and assess that learning? What are the teacher's criteria and standards? One of the most promising approaches to teacher self-assessment is the teaching portfolio (Edgerton, Hutchings, and Quinlan, 1991; Anderson, 1993; Seldin, 1991; and Chapter Nine of this volume).

Qualities best assessed by students. Students are, of course, the indisputable experts on how they perceive teachers and teaching, and on how instruction affects them. No one knows better than students if an instructor motivates or discourages them. Students are also good judges of how much they learn from instructors (Cashin, 1988). Therefore, student ratings of teaching can provide one very important indicator of teaching effectiveness if we ask the right questions.

Qualities best assessed by peers in the discipline. What students cannot assess well is whether they are learning enough of the "right" content and skills, fast enough, or well enough from a given teacher. To assess these criteria, assessment of course material and procedures by other teachers within the same discipline is needed. In the best case, from my viewpoint, students' work is also tested and evaluated by faculty other than those who taught the students.

Qualities best assessed by campus colleagues. Colleagues from the same campus but different disciplines are often the best assessors of whether the teaching in a particular department is consistent with an institution's overall mission, goals, and practices. Their perspective is especially important for the teaching in general education or core curriculum courses. Across the country, at all types of institutions, a great deal of promising work is being done on the review of teaching by peers from both the same and different disciplines (Shulman, 1993), work that is beginning to bear fruit in terms of prototype materials, resources, and tentative guidelines for good practice (Hutchings, 1995).

Assessment over Time. Even the best assessment instruments are subject to measurement error caused by variations in the assessment conditions. In a single-observation system, colleagues can easily visit a class on its single best or single worst day in an entire semester. To avoid this error, assessment needs to be ongoing involving several visits, for example, to determine consistency of performance.

A Community for Reflective Practice and Judgment. While research on teaching, learning, and assessment can help us identify critical criteria and indicators and offer guidelines for good practice, neither research nor guidelines can tell a particular department or institution which criteria or indicators to focus on or exactly how to apply the guidelines. Assessing and evaluating teaching effectively requires knowledge of and sensitivity to the individuals and groups involved, the local context, and the academic and administrative culture of the institution. In short, it requires the exercise of professional judgment. No teaching assessment or evaluation plan, however well-conceived, can work well if the faculty who are to carry out the assessment and be the assessors do not take it seriously. Therefore, effective teaching assessment requires the *collective* exercise of professional judgment.

In the past few years, Parker Palmer (1993), Lee Shulman (1993), and others have written eloquently about the need for and growing interest in reflective teaching, meaningful conversations about teaching, and the development of a sense of community among teachers. To effectively assess, evaluate, and improve college teaching requires a high level of trust, and a shared language and shared values related to teaching and learning. It requires, in short, that we develop communities of reflective practice and judgment.

Conclusion

At the most basic level, assessment is a powerful way to focus attention. This means that if I assess and evaluate teaching systematically, faculty are likely to pay more attention to teaching in general and, in particular, to focus more attention and effort on the specific criteria and indicators being assessed. This news is potentially good or bad. The good news is that if we focus our teaching assessments on the practices that actually lead to improved learning, we are likely to improve learning. The bad news is that if we focus on the wrong aspects, we are likely to trivialize assessment efforts, undermine good teaching, and impede learning. In any attempt to identify, assess, and honor exemplary teaching, the stakes are high. That makes it all the more incumbent on us to base our efforts on the best current research and practice. While what we *do not* know *can* hurt us, it is equally true that what others *do* know can *help* us.

References

Anderson, E. (ed.). *Campus Use of the Teaching Portfolio: Twenty-Five Profiles.* Washington, D.C.: American Association for Higher Education, 1993.

Angelo, T. A. "A Teacher's Dozen: Fourteen General, Research-Based Principles for Improving Higher Learning in Our Classrooms." *AAHE Bulletin,* 1993, *45* (8), 3–7, 13.

Astin, A. W., and others. "Principles of Good Practice for Assessing Student Learning." Washington, D.C.: American Association for Higher Education, 1992.

Barsi, L. M. "Some Illustrative Vignettes on the Uses of the Seven Principles and the Faculty and Institutional Inventories." In A. W. Chickering and Z. F. Gamson (eds.), *Applying the Seven Principles for Good Practice in Undergraduate Education.* New Directions for Teaching and Learning, no. 47. San Francisco: Jossey-Bass, 1991.

Braskamp, L. A., and Ory, J. C. *Assessing Faculty Work: Enhancing Individual and Institutional Performance.* San Francisco: Jossey-Bass, 1994.

Cashin, W. E. *Student Ratings of Teaching: A Summary of the Research.* Idea Paper No. 20. Manhattan: Center for Faculty Evaluation & Development, Kansas State University, 1988.

Cashin, W. E. *Defining and Evaluating College Teaching.* Idea Paper No. 21. Manhattan: Center for Faculty Evaluation & Development, Kansas State University, 1989.

Centra, J. A. *Reflective Faculty Evaluation: Enhancing Teaching and Determining Faculty Effectiveness.* San Francisco: Jossey-Bass, 1993.

Chickering, A. W., and Gamson, Z. F. (eds.). *Applying the Seven Principles for Good Practice in Undergraduate Education.* New Directions for Teaching and Learning, no. 47. San Francisco: Jossey-Bass, 1991.

Edgerton, R., Hutchings, P., and Quinlan, K. *The Teaching Portfolio: Capturing the Scholarship of Teaching.* Washington, D.C.: American Association for Higher Education, 1991.

Feldman, K. A. "Effective College Teaching from the Students' and Faculty's View: Matched or Mismatched Priorities?" *Research in Higher Education,* 1988, *28,* 291–344.

Gardiner, L. F. "Assessment Research, Evaluation, and Grading in Higher Education: Overview and Selected Resources." *Professional Resource No. 5.* Newark, N.J.: Rutgers University, 1995.

Hutchings, P. (ed.). *From Idea to Prototype: The Peer Review of Teaching: A Project Workbook.* Washington, D.C.: American Association for Higher Education, 1995.

Kahn, S. "Better Teaching Through Better Evaluation: A Guide for Faculty and Institutions." *To Improve the Academy,* 1993, *12,* pp. 111–126.

McKeachie, W. J., and others. *Teaching Tips: Strategies, Research, and Theory for College and University Teachers.* (9th ed.) Lexington, Mass.: Heath, 1994.

McKeachie, W. J., Pintrich, P. R., Lin, Y.-G., and Smith, D.A.F. *Teaching and Learning in the College Classroom: A Review of the Research Literature.* Ann Arbor: National Center to Improve Postsecondary Teaching and Learning, University of Michigan, 1986.

Palmer, P. J. "Good Talk About Good Teaching: Improving Teaching Through Conversation and Community." *Change,* 1993, 25 (6), 8–13.

Pascarella, E. T., and Terenzini, P. T. *How College Affects Students: Findings and Insights from Twenty Years of Research.* San Francisco: Jossey-Bass, 1991.

Seldin, P. *The Teaching Portfolio.* Bolton, Mass.: Anker, 1991.

Shulman, L. S. "Teaching as Community Property: Putting an End to Pedagogical Solitude." *Change,* 1993, 25 (6), 6–7.

Sorcinelli, M. D. "Research Findings on the Seven Principles." In A. W. Chickering and Z. F. Gamson (eds.), *Applying the Seven Principles for Good Practice in Undergraduate Education.* New Directions for Teaching and Learning, no. 47. San Francisco: Jossey-Bass, 1991.

Svinicki, M. D. "Practical Implications of Cognitive Theories." In R. J. Menges and M. D. Svinicki, (eds.), *College Teaching: From Theory to Practice.* New Directions for Teaching and Learning, no. 45. San Francisco: Jossey-Bass, 1991.

THOMAS A. ANGELO is director of the AAHE Assessment Forum, a core project of the American Association for Higher Education.

*To follow good measurement practice, programs for exemplary
teaching should gather more than one type of data from more than
one source. This practice is consistent with the idea behind the teaching
portfolio, a compilation of best work and thought that is gaining favor
as a faculty evaluation strategy.*

Using Portfolios to Document
Teaching Excellence

Laurie Richlin, Brenda Manning

Our experience with teaching portfolios as a means of documenting excellent
teaching has come from participating in the University of Pittsburgh's teaching
award process as mentors to nominees who create teaching portfolios and as
consultants to the judges who evaluate the portfolios. (A more detailed discussion of the University of Pittsburgh's Chancellor's Distinguished Teaching
Award is available from the authors.)

Few ideas are as appealing on the surface as encouraging professors to
gather and present for evaluation materials that best represent their teaching
excellence. Indeed, developing a teaching portfolio, or dossier, has become a
popular faculty development activity in many departments and on many campuses. To create portfolios, faculty select items such as syllabi, tests, student
work, and student evaluations about one or more courses and add a reflective
statement, often called a teaching philosophy, about their teaching goals. As
can be seen from descriptions in this volume, institutions may have specific or
general guidelines for what a portfolio should include and how the contents
will be evaluated (see, especially, Chapters Ten and Eleven).

Reactions to Constructing a Teaching Portfolio

In almost all cases, reports from our own faculty and from the field state that
professors find the teaching portfolio process reaffirming because it involves
them, perhaps for the first time, in self-reflection about their teaching. We have
seen that in most portfolio projects—regardless of source or situation—there
are faculty who enjoy and benefit from the portfolio-creation process itself. It is
often their first opportunity to document successes, to explain their teaching

struggles, and to find out that others have faced the same challenges with as much passion.

However, some professors decry the time and effort they put into constructing their portfolios when the work does not lead to their selection as award winners or to the promotions they anticipated. We believe this reaction occurs because of what we have *not* seen in evaluation projects using portfolios: a concurrent process to understand and express what constitutes excellent teaching and to develop a teaching evaluation system that reflects that understanding. Programs that use portfolios to make decisions for tenure, promotion, or honors seldom have guidelines for applying explicit criteria to those portfolios. Some report using what we term a *binary* system: they determine whether the professor did or did not engage in some activity determined to improve teaching, such as having a peer attend a class and write an evaluation. However, they do not have criteria to evaluate the activity itself. Other programs prefer to use a *generic* system, defining a good teacher through characteristics obtained from research (for instance, McKeachie and Cohen, 1980; McKeachie and others, 1994; Chapter Five, this volume), emphasizing such dimensions as mastery of content, organization, rapport with students, enthusiasm, and reflection on one's teaching. Unfortunately, definitions of what demonstrates those characteristics usually are no more explicit than the definitions in a binary system. It is assumed that judges or evaluators will "know it when they see it."

In most cases, it is not that there is *no* evaluation system (witness the wide range of selection processes described in this volume), but that the system is without agreed-upon and explicit criteria for judgment. *Without such agreed-upon and explicit criteria for judgment, we believe that faculty members are at risk should they submit their portfolios for evaluation for promotion and tenure and that judges are at risk in selecting the best award recipients.* As Menges points out in Chapter One, "Vagueness and secrecy foster suspicions about the objectivity and accuracy of the selection process."

Concerns with Current Evaluation Systems

We do not doubt that faculty evaluators (whether judges on a panel to choose outstanding teachers or department chairs deciding on promotion) are truly interested in recognizing teaching excellence. What has concerned us is that evaluators have no opportunity to work through their implicit beliefs about teaching in order to make explicit what they use as criteria for judging and selecting. Until those values are clearly stated, there can be no authentic decisions about how to evaluate teaching. Why is this the case? Recent research suggests that teaching is a highly individualized, context-dependent activity that can fruitfully be understood as a "profoundly ill-structured domain" (Shulman, 1992, p. 24), one in which many variables are at work and in which there are few clear-cut rules. Given the idiosyncratic character of discipline-based knowledge, it is most difficult to implement a set of measures that will provide sufficiently specific, descriptive information for judgments across departments. This means that for an evaluation-of-teaching system (ETS) to be useful for selecting outstanding teachers, it must be developed at the level (department, school, or campus) that is making the award. An ETS must provide rich, complex, formative, developmental, *nonstandardized* information (Braskamp and Ory, 1994). If nonstandardized information is to be valued, the traditional statistical evaluation approaches that exalt reliability and validity will not be enough. Institutions will need evaluation methods that can recognize, represent, and communicate the effectiveness with which a professor transforms discipline-based knowledge into teaching points and strategies that uniquely intersect with students' prior knowledge and their readiness and motivation to learn (Shulman, 1989). Institutions will need evaluation tools that can order and assign value to the many different dimensions of college teaching.

Because the goal of teaching is student learning (see Chapter Eight) and because students learn in many different ways, teachers look not for standardization but for *triangulation*. Accordingly, when teachers value the diverse learning needs of their students, their metaphor for reliability "changes from the National Bureau of Standards to that of a jury" of our peers (Shulman, personal conversation with one of the authors, January, 1995). Each student and faculty member is different; therefore, each of their evaluations may be personally valid yet differ from that of the others. To be as accurate as possible, it is necessary to base evaluation on many different standpoints. And that is what makes the diversity of materials in a teaching portfolio more reliable and valid for evaluation than the traditional single point of student evaluation data.

The drawback to the uniqueness of evaluation criteria is that to develop a useful and safe ETS, faculty members must bring their personal standpoint to bear on the development of their system. This is a time-consuming activity, and one in which most faculty are unprepared to participate. As a result of our own experiences and observations, we have created a curriculum through which a group can develop a *workable* ETS. An ETS that works must provide formative feedback, satisfy environmental demands, and honor the process of development by the faculty involved. Our decision to make that process a curriculum, as described below, has grown out of our realization that it takes time, study, and practice to make explicit the values implicit in teaching decisions.

Four Phases of Developing a Useful Evaluation-of-Teaching System

To guide efforts for developing a useful ETS, we have developed a four-phase curriculum with over 100 assignments to be completed individually or as a group (Richlin and Manning, 1995). The curriculum is divided into two main courses: *Teaching Portfolio 101 & 102* and *Peer Review 101 & 102*. The developmental assignments lead faculty from the personal, private development of their criteria for teaching excellence through group discussions of basic educational issues and the design of a pilot ETS to the safe tryout and redesign of that system. We see no shortcuts to this process, whether followed by a single department or a multicampus system. This has important implications for those involved in orienting new evaluators or judges.

Teaching Portfolio 101: Developing Personal Criteria. Faculty begin by working *in private* on a course portfolio (Cerbin, 1994), the first stage of a teaching portfolio. We ask faculty to start with a course portfolio, because "the courses we design and teach can properly be seen as a lens or window through which one may glimpse our discipline and its work" (Shulman, 1993, p. 13). We believe that private work on a personal portfolio, focused through the detailed knowledge each faculty member has about his or her courses, is the easiest and fastest way to identify an individual's goals and values in teaching. All the necessary material is close at hand or is an easily completed natural extension of that available material. Thus, the evaluation process begins with the faculty member's knowing his or her *own* criteria for what is good practice.

Important to this phase is the writing of reflective memos to what we call the "intelligent non-expert," who may be someone from another department who is serving on an institutionwide promotion or tenure committee or on a judge's panel for honoring an outstanding teacher. For the course they choose, faculty write memos explaining the syllabus, student assignments, student work, and student feedback. The very process of selecting material for inclusion is an expression of each faculty member's criteria for good teaching. The memos begin to make faculty aware of their own criteria in a form they will be able to share with their colleagues later on.

As faculty members become able to articulate and communicate their own values and goals—what is valid for them in their teaching—they will be able to identify the kinds of developmental information they would like to have to refine and improve their courses. Their private work will prepare them for academic unit or disciplinary conversations about what constitutes good practice in teaching in that unit or discipline (the focus of the next phase).

Teaching Portfolio 102: Discussing "Innocent" Issues. During the second phase of the first course, faculty members create a portfolio on second courses, including another set of reflective memos, and add an overarching teaching philosophy statement that combines what they have learned from each course. This work continues to be done privately. During the same time, the academic unit begins to work together, but *not directly on evaluation-of-teaching issues.* Assignments are carefully focused on a small number of key topics. The balance of private and public work reflects the belief that most people need time to reflect before they are ready to practice expressing their values and decisions about teaching.

The topics for group discussions are deceptively simple. Yet they lead inevitably to the heart of what is important to the faculty members about teaching and learning in their disciplines. Faculty often are surprised that during this phase they find themselves thinking about what they hoped when they first began to teach or first came to teach in this department. They may feel some anger and sadness when they realize the compromises they make to continue the balancing act that is college teaching today. The purpose of the public discussions is to identify the group's idea of excellence in teaching and to harness the emotional commitment the members have to that ideal. No one will, of course, get everything he or she wants. But each voice will contribute; one must speak to be heard.

Peer Review 101: Considering Elements of the Review Process. In the second course, faculty and administrators begin the delicate process of negotiating and designing an ETS that will fit their academic unit and institution. It is our assertion that all teaching units already have an ETS. However, in many, if not most, institutions, that ETS is based on convention or tradition rather than formal policy, and it may not be easy to find out what the existing system is.

The first task for participants in this phase is to identify the system that actually exists. The major decision elements include the faculty involved (what groups are evaluated similarly), purpose of the evaluation, reviewers of the material, material to be required, training for evaluation, written criteria, measurement level, and communication and feedback processes. If the group decides to include either in-class or videotaped observation in its system, there is a similar decision grid for implementing teaching observation. Elements in that grid include the observer(s), number of visits, training for observation, written criteria, measurement, and communication and feedback processes.

When they have decided on the material to be evaluated, faculty need to decide among three possible types of measurement systems: qualitative, ranked, or quantitative. In the qualitative systems, evaluators write a simple narrative about each item in a portfolio. In the ranked system, evaluators decide whether material is *unsatisfactory, satisfactory,* or *outstanding,* and write a simple narrative describing why. In the quantitative system, the evaluator assigns an agreed-upon number of points to each item, based on explicit criteria. Assignments in this phase are designed to aid faculty in finding their level of comfort in evaluating colleagues' work.

Peer Review 102: Testing and Revising the System. The final phase provides the opportunity for faculty members and administrators to test and revise their new system, based on their own portfolios and those of their colleagues. Instructors evaluate their own portfolios, first, providing written commentary based on the unit's ETS. They then work with two colleagues and provide both written and verbal feedback based on the materials. After testing the ETS, the group reassembles to refine and revise the system before it is formally implemented.

Conclusion

In order for those responsible for evaluating teaching portfolios (for any purpose) to be able to work together with agreed-upon criteria, they need to have taken the time to make explicit their teaching values. Evaluators and judges must be willing to work through the complexity of the teaching-learning experience.

For faculty striving for teaching excellence and those who wish to honor them, there are no shortcuts around the developmental process. A workable ETS requires time, attention, effort, and resources to achieve. Smith and Walvoord, in their call for national criterion-referenced certification (Chapter Three), point out that the implementation of an evaluation system requires time because it is a political as well as scientific process. Faculty and administrators interested in rewarding excellence in teaching need to use their knowledge of personal and community values, ideas, alternatives, and dreams to create a system that works.

References

Braskamp, L. A., and Ory, J. C. *Assessing Faculty Work: Enhancing Individual and Institutional Performance.* San Francisco: Jossey-Bass, 1994.

Cerbin, W. "The Course Portfolio for Continuous Improvement of Teaching and Learning." *Journal on Excellence in College Teaching,* 1994, 5 (1), 95–105.

McKeachie, W. J., and others. *Teaching Tips: Strategies, Research, and Theory for College and University Teachers.* (9th ed.) Lexington, Mass.: Heath, 1994.

McKeachie, W. J., and Cohen, P. C. "The Role of Colleagues in the Evaluation of College and University Teaching." *Improving College and University Teaching,* 1980, 28 (4), 147–154.

Richlin, L., and Manning, B. *Improving a College/University Teaching Evaluation System: A Comprehensive, Developmental Curriculum for Faculty & Administrators.* (2nd ed.) Pittsburgh: Alliance, 1995.

Shulman, L. "Toward a Pedagogy of Substance." *AAHE Bulletin,* 1989, 41 (10), 8–13.

Shulman, L. "Toward a Pedagogy of Cases." In J. H. Seulman (ed.), *Case Methods in Teacher Education.* New York: Teachers College Press, 1992.

Shulman, L. "Displaying Teaching to a Community of Peers." Paper presented at the AAHE National Conference on Faculty Roles and Rewards, San Antonio, Tex., Jan. 1993.

LAURIE RICHLIN is director of the Office of Faculty Development at the University of Pittsburgh, president of the International Alliance of Teacher Scholars, executive editor of the Journal on Excellence in College Teaching, *editor of the POD* Teaching Excellence *series, and director of the regional Lilly Conferences on College Teaching.*

BRENDA MANNING is associate director of the Office of Faculty Development at the University of Pittsburgh and frequent leader of portfolio development workshops for faculty and teaching assistants.

Faculty surveys and interviews suggest that such elements as input from faculty, administrators, and students and the provision of varied awards for good teaching are important to the success of recognition programs at research universities.

Honoring Exemplary Teaching in Research Universities

Mary Deane Sorcinelli, Barbara Gross Davis

In recent years, there has been increasing pressure on institutions of higher education to both improve and reward teaching. Within the academy as well, faculty, chairs, deans, and academic leaders have raised questions about the balance of rewards between teaching and research, particularly at research universities (Bok, 1991; Gray, Froh, and Diamond, 1992).

As administrators, we have each worked, on opposite coasts, for nearly two decades to develop at research universities, institutions that traditionally support the primacy of research and publication, a culture that values teaching. And while it remains a familiar complaint that teaching is not rewarded at research universities, a number of initiatives are in place or being piloted that promise, in concert, to better honor exemplary teaching. In particular, our experience confirms the importance of the "fit" of an award program with an institution's culture and context if teaching awards are to be a meaningful and significant part of the campus landscape.

In this chapter, we first discuss the most prevalent means of encouraging and rewarding excellence in teaching, namely, campuswide teaching awards. We outline key areas to consider in the development of such awards including the aspects of teaching honored, evidence on which selections are based, and processes for choosing those to be honored. Then we offer some suggestions from award recipients on how to improve the prizes. Finally we describe other incentives used at our and other large universities to honor and affirm teaching.

Nature of Teaching Awards

Teaching awards have been part of higher education for many years. For example, at the University of California, Berkeley, an institutional teaching award

NEW DIRECTIONS FOR TEACHING AND LEARNING, no. 65, Spring 1996 © Jossey-Bass Publishers

was first given in 1959. A similar program was launched in 1962 at the University of Massachusetts, Amherst. A recent study indicates that many colleges and universities have such awards, typically given to individuals on the basis of submitted materials documenting excellence in teaching (Miller, 1995). Usually an institution gives one to six awards annually, often with cash prizes, and recipients are typically honored at a public ceremony.

Criteria. What dimensions or characteristics of good teaching merit recognition? Other chapters in this volume address this question in greater depth. However, our belief is that teaching awards tend often reflect local guidelines and definitions of excellence. For example, at our universities, teaching and research are both essential duties of the faculty, and distinguished teaching awards acknowledge the efforts of faculty members who have successfully united these two roles. Lecturers are judged on their excellence in teaching and their contributions to the teaching mission of the university.

Specific criteria at University of California, Berkeley, include: command of the subject, continuous growth in the field of study, ability to organize course material and to present it cogently, effective design and redesign of courses, ability to inspire in students independent and original thinking, ability to encourage intellectual interests in beginning students and to stimulate creative work in advanced students, enthusiasm and vitality in learning and teaching, guidance of student research projects, participation in advising students, participation in guiding and supervising graduate student instructors (teaching assistants), and ability to respond to a diverse study body. At University of Massachusetts, Amherst, the criteria are similar and surveys of other research universities have found, in nearly all cases, the use of some combination of the aforementioned dimensions of teaching (Miller, 1995; Quinn, 1994).

Nomination and Review Process. The University of Massachusetts, Amherst, and many other campuses administer their award programs through a one-stage process: nominations are solicited by a certain date, the committee holds a series of meetings to review the submissions and makes its decisions. University of California, Berkeley, used to employ such a process but changed its procedures in 1992. The reasons for the change are instructive. By the late 1980s, the number of submissions for the award had grown to twenty to twenty-five (for three to five annual awards), and many excellent teachers and their departments felt great frustration about not being selected. In addition, the size of the dossiers and materials submitted (letters, evaluation data, teaching materials, statements from the nominee and from the nominating committee and department chair) placed a burden on the Academic Senate Committee on Teaching whose members devoted three to six hours to reviewing a single submission.

Under the new system, the award is a two-stage process. In stage one, departments initiate nominations by submitting a letter of no more than four single-spaced pages, from a department representative; a summary (qualitative, numerical, or both) of the nominee's teaching evaluations for all courses taught during the last eight semesters of residence; and raw student evaluation data from any two courses offered by the nominee in the most recent four semesters of residence. All three requisites can be filled without consulting the candidate, and these stage one nominations are made confidentially.

The Academic Senate Committee on Teaching reviews the stage one nominations and selects approximately ten submissions for further consideration. In stage two, the original submission is supplemented by the candidate's brief statement of his or her teaching philosophy; the candidate's curriculum vitae; no more than fifteen letters of support, including letters from campus colleagues, current students, and former students; raw student evaluation data from two additional courses in the four-semester period; and supporting materials (syllabi, tests, graded assignments, and so on) for any two of the four courses for which student evaluations are being submitted.

These changes have had the effect of minimizing the amount of work for departments, reducing the number of disappointed faculty, and decreasing the workload for the review committee.

How to Improve Teaching Award Programs

The following suggestions for improving teaching award programs are based on interviews with award-winning faculty at five research universities, including both of our campuses (Quinn, 1994), as well as surveys of faculty at other institutions (McNaught and Anwyl, 1992; Miller, 1995).

Clearly State and Widely Publicize the Selection Process. It is important that the awards be seen not as a display of in-group favoritism nor a cosmetic gesture nor an exercise in public relations. Thus, the campus should issue a clear statement of eligibility, criteria for teaching excellence, deadlines for nominations, and the nomination and selection procedures. It helps, too, to have a well-respected group make the awards; for example, an academic senate committee of senior faculty members with broad experience or a committee of former distinguished teaching award winners.

Make Peer, Administrator, and Especially Student Input an Important Part of the Process. As has been discussed in earlier chapters, the fullest picture of an individual's teaching emerges from a wide array of data. Information from students can be collected through end-of-course questionnaires, special surveys, letters, and interviews. Colleagues can evaluate course materials and observe classes to judge an instructor's mastery of course content, organization, and appropriate use of instructional materials. Instructors can be asked to submit a statement about their methods, goals, and accomplishments (Sorcinelli, 1986).

Provide More and Different Kinds of Recognition for Good Teaching. It is quite common for distinguished teachers to be honored in a public ceremony with both campus and external media coverage. Such ceremonies are valuable in demonstrating, both to internal and external constituencies, that the campus values teaching as an academic activity. Campuses can also spotlight teaching by asking award-winning faculty to facilitate workshops for other faculty, offer a "distinguished lecture" on teaching, or serve as a master teacher or mentor for new faculty.

Many campuses also connect teaching awards to such long-term rewards as tenure, promotion, and merit increases. For example, at University of California, Berkeley, the Academic Senate personnel committee that reviews all merit raises and promotions on campus instituted a policy in 1991 that gives senior faculty members a one-step increase for meritorious teaching. Because receiving the teaching award is considered evidence of meritorious teaching, this policy has served both to recognize the importance of the award and enhance its prestige.

Creating Other Incentives to Sustain Good Teaching

Campuswide teaching awards do highlight outstanding teaching, but announcing a handful of awards each year does not directly acknowledge the large number of faculty members who are committed to excellence in teaching. To more broadly reaffirm the value of teaching, and to recognize and support innovation, campuses can move beyond a once-a-year ceremony.

Offer More Awards for Excellent Teachers. In addition to presenting one major campuswide teaching award, some universities have established smaller and more diverse award programs. For example, the University of Massachusetts, Amherst, recently instituted a College Outstanding Teacher Award to augment the campus's distinguished teaching awards. Each of the university's colleges and schools selects one or two outstanding faculty members each year, who receive a cash award ($1,000) and a commemorative plaque. They are also featured in the campus newspaper and recognized at undergraduate commencement exercises.

The University of California, Berkeley, also has a program of encouraging local recognition at the departmental and college level. In addition, there are discipline-specific awards that cut across departments (for example, the Noyce award for excellence in teaching in the physical sciences).

Another innovative reward for teaching is the Faculty Associate Program, developed by the Center for Teaching at the University of Massachusetts, Amherst. Faculty associates are drawn from the ranks of former teaching award recipients and receive release time from one course per year for two years to offer center-sponsored workshops, collaborate on special projects, and act as general consultants throughout the academic year. Other campuses provide rotating endowed chairs for distinguished teachers (each chair held for a specific number of years), "master teacher" awards, and "distinguished mentor" or "outstanding advisor" awards.

Create Teaching Communities and Rewards for Departments and Colleges. Campus leaders at some research universities have urged that the focus of incentives for good teaching be broadened from individual faculty members to departments. A number of universities have inaugurated teaching awards to departments to emphasize the cooperative nature of university teaching (Wergin, 1993).

At the University of California, Berkeley, the Educational Initiatives Award (carrying $10,000) is given to a department or unit that makes a distinctive contribution to undergraduate education by creating "an outstanding program or initiative that could serve as a model for other departments." Qualifying initiatives include major curricular reform, exemplary advising or mentoring programs, major overhaul of service courses, enhanced research opportunities for undergraduates, and innovative use of graduate student instructors.

In order to encourage departmental initiatives aimed at improving undergraduate education, enhancing a multicultural environment, and better preparing graduate students for careers that include teaching, the dean of the College of Humanities and Fine Arts at the University of Massachusetts, Amherst, offers annual prizes of $5,000 for each of the following: the best departmental proposal to improve the quality or delivery of instruction or services to undergraduates, the best departmental proposal to extend the curriculum into new cultural areas or to support students and teachers who venture into these new areas, and the best departmental proposal to improve the preparation or evaluation of graduate students as teachers.

Develop an Active Academy of Distinguished Teachers. To sustain a sense of community and enthusiasm among award-winning faculty, some campuses convene the distinguished teachers to undertake special projects or advise and consult on issues facing the campus (see Chapter Four). For example, the group of distinguished teachers at Berkeley has met periodically to provide leadership in teaching and instruction. At the University of Massachusetts, Amherst, the chancellor has just initiated an annual reception for distinguished teaching–award winners in order to seek their advice on teaching matters.

Publicize the Achievements of Exemplary Teachers. Many campuses publicize profiles of recipients of the teaching award. At the University of California, Berkeley, essays about good teaching written by distinguished teachers as part of their nomination for the award have been compiled into *What Good Teachers Say About Teaching* (Tollefson and Davis, 1994).

At the University of Massachusetts, considerable publicity is also given to distinguished teaching award recipients through the campus newspaper, local newspapers, the alumni magazine, and other university publications. In addition, the campus's Center for Teaching highlights selected teaching award winners as facilitators in its annual series of campuswide workshops and seminars.

Provide Additional Support for Innovations in Teaching. Institutional commitment can also be expressed through modest financial awards made to faculty members interested in improving a course or the teaching of it. Our informal surveys indicate that many research universities, including our own, award a range of faculty grants for teaching development.

For example, the University of Massachusetts, Amherst, annually awards Faculty Grants for Teaching, Multicultural Initiatives, and Service Learning Grants to encourage faculty to explore new approaches to instruction. Each program has different criteria and review processes as well as varying resources to assist grantees in completing their projects. Grants are small—no more than $2,000—but often provide the seed money that leads to matching funds from other internal or external sources.

At University of California, Berkeley, avenues for innovation in teaching include the Minigrant, Classroom Technology, and Service Learning grant programs for faculty. Each program has different criteria and levels of funding, for example, the maximum award for a minigrant is $1,000, for a classroom technology grant, $3,500.

Conclusion

This chapter has offered some practical steps for administering teaching awards programs and creating other incentives for excellence in teaching. Of course, no one prize or activity in itself is sufficient to convey a campus's commitment to teaching. But when institutions recognize outstanding faculty or groups of faculty, they do more than merely honor individuals. They set standards for emulation and signal campus ideals. A strong network of incentives and rewards for good teaching thus contributes to campus values and cultures. At the Universities of California and Massachusetts and at other research universities, much is being done to affirm the theme that teaching and research are complementary—not competing—aspects of professional life.

References

Bok, D. "The Improvement of Teaching." *Teachers' College Record,* 1991, *93* (2), 236–251.

Davis, B. G. *Tools for Teaching.* San Francisco: Jossey-Bass, 1993.

Gray, P. J., Froh, R. C., and Diamond, R. M. *A National Study of Research Universities on the Balance Between Research and Undergraduate Teaching.* Syracuse, N.Y.: Center for Instructional Development, Syracuse University, 1992.

McKeachie, W. J., and others. *Teaching Tips: Strategies, Research, and Theory for College and University Teachers.* (9th ed.) Lexington, Mass.: Heath, 1994.

McNaught, C., and Anwyl, J. *Awards for Teaching Excellence at Australian Universities.* Centre for the Study of Higher Education Research Working Papers 93.1. Melbourne, Aust.: Melbourne University, 1992.

Miller, E. "Rewarding Faculty for Teaching Excellence/Effectiveness: A Survey of Currently Available Awards Including Faculty Comments and Desires in Regard to the Process of Rewards." Unpublished doctoral dissertation, Texas A&M University, 1995.

Quinn, J. W. "Teaching Award Recipients' Perceptions of Teaching Award Programs." Paper presented at the Second AAHE Forum on Faculty Roles and Rewards, New Orleans, Jan. 1994.

Sorcinelli, M. D. *Evaluation of Teaching Handbook.* Bloomington, Ind.: Indiana University Press, 1986.

Tollefson, S. K., and Davis, B. G. *What Good Teachers Say About Teaching: Essays from Berkeley.* Berkeley: Office of Educational Development, University of California, 1994.

Wergin, J. "Departmental Awards." *Change,* 1993, *22* (4), 24.

MARY DEANE SORCINELLI *is associate provost for faculty development and director of the Center for Teaching, University of Massachusetts, Amherst*

BARBARA GROSS DAVIS *is assistant vice chancellor, educational development, at the University of California, Berkeley.*

Two-year colleges have consistently led the way in developing the teaching mission of higher education; a survey shows how these teaching institutions are responding to the need to honor their teachers.

Honoring Exemplary Teaching: The Two-Year College Setting

Mardee Jenrette, Karen Hays

In 1988, the American Association of Community and Junior Colleges Commission on the Future of Community Colleges issued *Building Communities: A Vision for a New Century.* This report, which has become a blueprint document for numerous two-year colleges, states in part, "Teaching is the heartbeat of the educational enterprise and, when it is successful, energy is pumped into the community, continuously renewing and revitalizing the institution" (pp. 7–8). It goes on to say that, "excellence in teaching should be honored. . . . Programs to acknowledge teaching excellence should be established at every community college" (p. 27).

Two-year colleges are mindful of their heritage and profess to take their teaching mission seriously. They proudly claim *the nation's premier teaching institutions* as their higher education niche. However, data collected in a 1989–1990 Higher Education Research Institute study of 35,000 faculty in 392 public institutions of higher education raise some questions about support of that mission (Higher Education Research Institute, 1992). While it may not be surprising that only 6.2 percent of university faculty found the statement, "faculty are rewarded for being good teachers" very descriptive of their institutions, that only 8 percent of community college faculty found the attribute descriptive of *their* institutions is a surprise.

The objectives of this chapter are to address the extent to which and manner in which U.S. two-year colleges currently recognize and honor exemplary teaching and to offer observations that may be useful when institutions are assessing or implementing recognition programs. To achieve the former objective, the results of a national survey will be described. Although we consider the data preliminary—not an exhaustive review of colleges' efforts to encourage exemplary teaching—they do provide a national perspective on the types of recognition currently extended to full- and part-time faculty for their teaching, who makes the decisions to recognize certain faculty, and how these decisions are made.

Surveys were mailed to academic officers at two-year colleges across the country. Of the 1,216 surveys mailed, 346 (28 percent) were returned by early June 1995. (A copy of the survey is available from the authors.) Colleges were invited to provide descriptive materials about their programs along with their survey responses.

Institutional Demographics

A majority of the surveys returned were from institutions that employ one hundred or fewer full-time faculty (61.4 percent), the fewest were from those with over six hundred full-time faculty (1.2 percent). Almost half of the institutions (47.7 percent) that responded employ up to one hundred adjunct faculty and 5.2 percent employ over six hundred adjunct faculty. Most of the faculty (60.1 percent) in the responding institutions are not unionized.

Programs to Honor Exemplary Teaching

Most responding colleges (68.7 percent) currently offer one or more programs to recognize exemplary teaching, while 45.4 percent of those that do not have plans to do so. Only 26.9 percent of the colleges, however, have formally defined exemplary teaching in a policy or a procedure.

Certificates and plaques are the most common type of awards given to full-time faculty, although 54.6 percent of the 346 institutions offer more than one type of recognition. Travel opportunities and attendance at conferences (41 percent) and monetary awards (40 percent) are also given. Sixteen (5 percent) of the responding colleges have endowed teaching chairs.

Of those institutions with programs to honor exemplary teaching, nearly half (47.8 percent) recognize up to 2 percent of their full-time faculty annually. Thirty percent recognize 3 to 5 percent of their faculty annually, 14.2 percent honor 6 to 10 percent, and 8.1 percent honor more than 10 percent.

Exemplary adjunct faculty are recognized at 42.6 percent of responding colleges. Again, the most common award is a certificate or plaque (26 percent); however, 12 percent of the colleges provide travel opportunities and attendance at conferences, and 12 percent provide monetary awards. Sixty institutions (56 percent) of those that recognize adjunct teachers offer more than one type of recognition.

These preliminary survey results indicate no significant relationship between the size of the institution as measured by the number of full-time faculty and the presence of programs to honor exemplary teaching. It appears that larger institutions are more likely to offer such programs; however, the number of respondents is too small to speak definitively. Further, there seems to be no relationship between faculty unionization and the existence of such programs.

Decision Making

Faculty colleagues are most often part of the process to identify exemplary teachers. However, at approximately 49.7 percent of responding colleges a combination of faculty, administrators, students, and community members or others (such as alumni or foundation members) plays a role in decision making.

Nomination letters from staff members, administrators, faculty, or students or self-nomination letters from the candidates themselves are used most consistently (at 70.6 percent of the responded colleges) to initiate the process. Approximately 47.3 percent of survey respondents indicated that a combination of nomination letters, portfolios, and/or applications is used as supporting documentation in decision making.

Institutional Benefits

The survey provided an opportunity for academic officers to express their views on institutional benefits derived from programs to recognize exemplary teaching. Many respondents identified one or more of the following: the positive effect on student learning, the elevation of faculty morale, the reestablishment of an institutional focus on teaching, the encouragement and promotion of high-quality instruction, positive publicity for the college, the encouragement of ongoing professional development, and the recognition of individual teachers (and thus the college) at national, state, or local events.

Audit of Practices to Honor Exemplary Teaching

Through its written policies and procedures, its customary practices, and the day-to-day behaviors of its principal constituencies, the climate and values of an institution are revealed. O'Banion (1994) suggests an audit of the foregoing as an important first step for leaders who wish to make teaching and learning their highest priority. With faculty as "the conjunction that connects the teaching *and* learning processes" (p. 312), institutional practices relating to faculty are prominent among O'Banion's audit guidelines. The key questions he sees in assessing institutional rewards include these: Are the most effective teachers being rewarded? Are the rewards appropriate to the achievement? Are the reward mechanisms such that those not recognized respect the process and outcomes? We offer the following questions as an extension of that audit of practices to recognize exemplary teaching. In a number of cases, we have used examples submitted by survey respondents as illustrations.

1. *Is there agreement among constituencies within the college on what constitutes exemplary teaching? How far out of the classroom does "teaching" extend?* Bainbridge

College, Georgia, answers the question, "What is Good Teaching at Bainbridge College?" with a description of nine activity categories. Miami-Dade Community College, Florida, has published "Statement of Faculty Excellence," a narrative document describing twenty-nine qualities of the excellent faculty member. Both descriptions address classroom work but recognize that continued professional development, research, publishing, activity in professional organizations, and college and community service contribute to good teaching.

2. *Are criteria for selecting award recipients clear? Are they derived from a commonly held concept of exemplary teaching?* Albuquerque Technical-Vocational Institute, New Mexico, includes in nomination brochures its "Philosophy of Learning/Teaching," which incorporates eighteen activities engaged in by its teachers. Corning Community College, New York, in the application for its Board of Trustees Excellence in Teaching Award, elaborates in detail five criteria that define excellent performance.

3. *How is the applicant pool for an award created?* The vast majority of colleges use a nomination process. Nominators range from recent alumni (Kirkwood Community College, Iowa) to students and employees (Cuyahoga Community College, Ohio), groups of nominators (Monroe Community College, New York), and even the nominees themselves (Isothermal Community College, North Carolina and Miami-Dade Community College).

4. *Who makes the decision? Who is in the best position to judge exemplary teaching?* Practices include committees of students, faculty, and previous winners (Dallas Community College District, Texas), only previous winners (Western Piedmont Community College, North Carolina), boards of trustees (Seattle Community College, Washington) or external judges (Johnson County Community College, Kansas). Some institutions use a voting procedure (Palo Alto College, Texas: faculty; Delta College, Michigan: students past and present; Bakersfield College, California: students). Sometimes decision makers or award bestowers are external: the National Institute for Staff and Organizational Development, which offers a Teaching Excellence Award, and the North Carolina Department of Community Colleges, which offers an Educator of the Year award, are examples.

5. *Are award recipients selected through competitive or standards-driven processes? And once an award is given, is the recipient eligible for it again?* The vast majority of recognition programs in existence today are based on a competitive model. Miami-Dade Community College has no "sit-out" time for an endowed chair, but limits a chair applicant's portfolio to accomplishments since his or her last award. For other colleges, five years seems to be a common length of time for a required sit-out. It is stipulated by the Dallas Community College District, Western Piedmont Community College, and Cuyahoga Community College, among others. At Herkimer County Community College, New York, and Honolulu Community College, Hawaii, past recipients are not eligible for an award.

6. *Are awards "duty free," or do they carry an obligation? Is recognition for past accomplishments or future plans?* On the one hand, the Miami-Dade Com-

munity College endowed teaching chair is given in recognition of past performance; the recipient is only required to maintain faculty status during the period of time (three years) the chair is held. On the other hand, Delta College provides its endowed chair recipients with funds to complete a project, and at Broward Community College, Florida, a portion of the award is for a similar purpose. Isothermal Community College proposes to "reward outstanding service and to support its continuation." Calhoun State Community College, Alabama, requires recipients of its teaching award "to share that excellence with colleagues, students, and members of the community." Corning Community College, New York, gives its board of trustees excellence award in recognition of past performance; however, recipients must undertake a project and share the results with colleagues.

7. *Must the teacher have proven his or her exemplary skills in classrooms of the college making the award?* Bakersfield College requires ten years of prior college service of its distinguished teaching/leadership honorees. Trinity Valley Community College, Texas, specifies two years of service for its excellence in teaching award.

8. *Are the awards of sufficient value to be motivating? Are there sufficient numbers of awards that those not yet recognized can continue to find them motivating?* The Dallas Community College District gives $2,000 to the full-time faculty member receiving its Miles Production Company Outstanding Faculty Award and $1000 each to the six semifinalists. In addition, one adjunct faculty member on each of the seven Dallas campuses receives $200 for professional expenditures. Isothermal's four endowed chairs each carry $2,500 for approved expenses. Broward Community College's five professors of the year attend a conference of their choice, while each of its thirty endowed chair recipients receives an annual $5,000 salary bonus and $2,500 for expenses for a three-year period. Each recipient of Miami-Dade's one hundred endowed chairs receives a similar $22,500 in salary enhancement and expenses over three years.

9. *Are award recipients widely publicized?* Western Piedmont announces its Excellence in Teaching Award at spring commencement. Rancho Santiago College, California, publishes "Profiles in Excellence," which features a series of award winners, and the Distinguished Faculty Award winner delivers a public address that is published and distributed to colleges throughout the state of California. Butler County Community College, Kansas, sponsors a "Celebrating Excellence" ceremony and reception at which various awards are given. Hartford Community College, Maryland, honors recipients at its opening faculty meeting.

10. *Is the recognition of exemplary teaching limited to awards to exemplary practitioners?* Numerous institutions work to develop as well as reward exemplary teachers and to create environments that support exemplary teaching. The Middlesex Community College, Massachusetts, Faculty and Staff Development Program provides minigrants, targeted curriculum development programs, and publications and activities presented for faculty by faculty. William Rainey Harper College, Illinois, funds a number of teaching and learning initiatives.

Dallas County Community College District has a "Reading Room" of print and nonprint resources, while Cuyahoga's program features a faculty lecture series and a scholar-in-residence. Teaching and learning centers to support teaching excellence are a growing trend in community colleges. Thriving examples may be found at the County College of Morris, New Jersey; De Anza College, California; Florida Community College at Jacksonville; the Maricopa Community Colleges, Arizona; Chemeketa Community College, Oregon; Golden West College, California; Johnson County Community College, Kansas; and Miami-Dade Community College, Florida.

Conclusion

The following observations about honoring exemplary teaching in two-year colleges are based on our preliminary survey data, the literature, and our experience. We are certain readers will have additional observations of their own.

1. *Virtually all community colleges claim to be teaching institutions first, yet one-third of our sample does not honor exemplary teaching.*

2. *While nearly 70 percent of respondents at two-year colleges reported that they reward excellent teachers, only 8 percent of their faculty seem to agree.* One can only speculate on the discrepancy; however, when very few rewards are given, even an outstanding teacher may feel he or she has no chance to be recognized. Substantial monetary rewards are limited by necessity, but all excellent teachers can be recognized, in some way, perhaps with a certificate, a plaque, a luncheon, or a photograph in a publication.

3. *When criteria for awards are not linked to a definition of exemplary teaching and/or made explicit, they may shift from year to year as decision makers change.* When standards change constantly, one opportunity to move an institution forward in its mission to promote exemplary teaching is lost.

4. *Relying too heavily on nomination by others for awards creates a risk that excellent candidates may be overlooked and/or that solicitation of nominations will demean the process.* In addition, the completion of a dauntingly complex nomination form says less about the exemplary teacher than it does about the nominator.

5. *Careful attention needs to be given to all factors that speak to the value of an award.* Intention, ultimately, does not matter if the recipient does not find the award of value. If the award is monetary, is the amount sufficient? Who are the other recipients? Are the decision makers knowledgeable enough to base the award on the right criteria?

6. *Two-year colleges employ large numbers of adjunct faculty who should also be recognized as excellent teachers.*

7. *Excellent work is rarely done in isolation; exemplary teaching is frequently the outcome of collaborative efforts.* Therefore, honoring departments can be a productive focus.

8. *Institutions should not lose sight of the fact that it is possible to recognize an individual and advance an institutional goal at the same time.* Communicating broadly who the exemplary teachers are helps them serve as models for colleagues. Treating *all* teachers well (that is, providing support for professional growth, evaluating performance fairly and honestly, creating a nonpunitive environment in which risk taking can occur, making the classroom the number one priority in budget decisions) is probably one of the most effective ways a community college can honor exemplary teaching.

References

American Association of Community and Junior Colleges. Commission on the Future of Community Colleges. *Building Communities: A Vision for a New Century.* Washington, D.C.: American Association of Community and Junior Colleges, 1988.

Higher Education Research Institute. "The American College Teacher: National Norms for the 1989–90 HERI Faculty Survey." *The Chronicle of Higher Education,* Aug. 26, 1992.

O'Banion, T. "Guidelines for Auditing the Effectiveness of Teaching and Learning." In T. O'Banion and Associates, *Teaching and Learning in The Community College.* Washington, D.C.: American Association of Community Colleges, 1994.

MARDEE JENRETTE *is dean for teaching/learning advancement at Miami-Dade Community College in Florida.*

KAREN HAYS *is the self-study director at Miami-Dade Community College.*

Liberal arts institutions have long been known for seeing teaching as a primary mission. Their methods for recognizing exemplary teaching are discussed in this chapter.

Honoring Exemplary Teaching in the Liberal Arts Institution

Kenneth J. Zahorski

From its very inception, the liberal arts institution has been defined by its primary mission of providing a quality education for undergraduate students. While scholarship has also been valued and rewarded, teaching has remained the focal point of the liberal arts enterprise, its very raison d'être. Thus, the liberal arts college is naturally expected to expend its energies and resources on teaching and on all the agents that nurture teaching, including practices that honor it. This chapter identifies some of the most common practices liberal arts institutions use to honor outstanding teaching and concludes with a set of recommendations for enhancing what is now being done.

Distinctiveness of Liberal Arts Institutions

While teaching is honored throughout academe, the methods are far from uniform. The type of institution can significantly affect how, and how well, recognition of effective teaching is provided. Four distinguishing features of the traditional liberal arts institution help determine the form and effectiveness of practices for honoring teaching in these colleges.

To begin with, the fundamental tenet of the liberal arts mission is that good teaching results in good learning. Anything less than a total commitment to fostering good teaching is a betrayal of the liberal arts credo. Because of their total commitment to fostering the teaching-learning enterprise, liberal arts colleges find it easier to support and reward pedagogy than institutions largely devoted to research. Second, most liberal arts institutions are relatively small, a trait that enables them to take a holistic, collegial approach toward honoring teaching. Third, and also owing to liberal arts colleges' relatively small size, student-faculty relationships are typically quite close; consequently, students are important sources of input for identifying exemplary teachers. Fourth, in liberal arts colleges, the centrality of community and collegiality, along with an emphasis upon cooperation and collaboration rather than competition, raises serious questions about the appropriateness of competitive teaching awards.

Common Honoring Practices

Following are introductory descriptions of some of the practices most frequently used to honor exemplary teaching in liberal arts colleges. The underlying concepts are then more concretely explored in the next section.

Outstanding Teaching Awards. Today, at least 70 percent of all college campuses have awards for teaching excellence (Smith and Walvoord, 1993). Although permutations abound, most teaching awards exhibit the following common denominators: usually only full-time faculty are eligible; nominations, accepted from faculty, students, and alumni, are reviewed by a selection committee consisting of faculty, administrators, and students; awards are presented at commencement ceremonies or some type of academic honors convocation; and awards are usually both honorary and monetary.

Mentoring Programs. One very practical yet effective method of recognizing outstanding teachers is to ask them to share their teaching acumen with colleagues new to the profession, often as part of an orientation program. While being asked to serve as mentor is an honor in itself, some programs build in opportunities for additional acknowledgement. At St. Norbert College, for example, mentors are honored at a Mentor Appreciation Dinner, during which new colleagues offer testimonials in recognition of the help their mentors have provided (Zahorski, 1994).

In-House Publications. Liberal arts institutions frequently honor exemplary teachers through articles and interviews in internal college publications ranging from student newspapers to faculty development newsletters. Each type of publication addresses a particular group or interest. Students are not only eager to discover excellent teachers but also pleased to see their favorite instructors recognized. Faculty are happy to see good teaching rewarded and are also interested in their honored colleagues' observations on pedagogy.

National Awards. While students and colleagues constitute the most important audience for teaching honorees, outside recognition is also important. Consequently, many liberal arts institutions regularly nominate their outstanding teachers for such prestigious national awards as the Carnegie Foundation for the Advancement of Teaching U.S. Professors of the Year and the American Association of Higher Education Exemplary Teaching Program. Such awards bring distinction not only to the individual recipient but also to his or her institution.

Merit Raises. Merit pay is a fairly common yet controversial form of honoring exemplary teaching. Faculty give merit increments mixed reviews, however. Their ambivalence stems not so much from the concept as from the often secretive and vague process by which merit increases are made.

Recommendations

I set forth the following recommendations in the spirit of sanguine exploration and with full knowledge that they are neither original nor definitive. Rather, I offer them as possible ways in which liberal arts institutions might take fuller advantage of their distinguishing traits as they attempt to honor exemplary teaching ever more effectively. Examples of recommended practices are taken from both liberal arts colleges and other higher education institutions.

Review Institutional Mission Statement. The first step in determining an institution's approach to honoring teaching should be a thorough review of the institutional mission statement. This must be done to ensure congruity between mission and reward, both in terms of the types of rewards offered and the process used to select recipients. For example, if the reexamination reveals that community and collegiality are central to the mission, some very important questions must be asked. Are competitive awards in keeping with the spirit of community? Does the selection process involve a broad base of faculty, resulting in a sense of shared ownership? Does the reward structure foster harmony and cooperation or divisiveness and competition? The answers to these kinds of basic questions will help determine the fundamental tenets that must undergird effective honoring practices for the institution.

Strengthen the Selection Process. Edgerton (1993) reminds us that "reservations about awards for teaching excellence begin with doubts that merit always prevails in the selection process" (p. 22). Most institutions, no matter how sound their selection guidelines, could probably enhance them through a careful examination. Such questions as the following might launch the review: Are the selection guidelines clearly articulated and easily accessible to the entire academic community? Are the selection criteria based upon an informed understanding of what constitutes good teaching? Are the selection criteria congruent with the institution's mission statement, tenure and promotion criteria, and teaching culture? Are faculty and students centrally involved in the selection process?

Whatever the questions, the goal should be to demystify the selection process and to enable the entire academic community to assume ownership of it.

Reconsider the Conventional Teaching Award. Despite the teaching award's widespread use, many have questioned its efficacy, and the litany of concern seems to be growing, as discussed in Chapter One.

The most serious indictment of the teaching award is not that it fails to achieve its full promise but that it actually does damage. Eble (1983), for example, laments that "single awards, such as for teacher of the year, are as much fomenters of discord as stimuli to good teaching" (pp. 130–131), a view shared by Frederick (Peter Frederick, telephone interview by the author,

Apr. 3, 1995). Others believe individual teaching awards can actually run counter to an institution's goal for "encouraging the notion of teaching as a highly collaborative and cooperative activity" (Timothy Riordan, correspondence with the author, Feb. 22, 1995).

Despite its drawbacks, the award concept has made a significant contribution to enriching the teaching cultures of many institutions. If nothing else, these awards succeeded in gaining for teaching a new visibility at a time when only scholarship was being recognized and rewarded.

Honor All Exemplary Teachers, Whether Full- or Part-Time. The vital concept of honoring *all* exemplary teachers, whether full- or part-time, is founded on two fundamental principles. First, a liberal arts institution's primary goal is to provide students with the best teaching possible, and this can be done only if *all* teachers are nurtured and rewarded equally. Second, all institutions of higher learning should make every effort to provide part-time colleagues with the rewards and benefits accorded full-time, tenure track faculty.

In response to the need for reward parity, some institutions have developed special awards for part-time and adjunct faculty. For example, each year at commencement, Boston University's Metropolitan College recognizes a part-time faculty member for teaching excellence (Office of Faculty and Program Development, Boston University Metropolitan College, n.d.) and at Bentley College, one of the two annual teaching awards goes to a part-time faculty member (Bentley College, 1994). Such special awards for adjunct and part-time faculty are a step in the right direction. But serious consideration ought to be given to an even more dramatic step—making part-time faculty eligible for all institutional teaching awards. This inclusive approach not only would be good for the teaching-learning enterprise but also would boost the morale of part-time colleagues, who often feel isolated from the academic community.

Honor All Kinds of Teaching. As important as making *all* faculty eligible for collegial recognition is honoring *all* kinds of teaching. That is, we must take pains to recognize those fine instructors "who are very good at quietly getting students to think for themselves and to learn how to learn on their own, [but who] might not be recognized as readily as the provocative lecturer or the socratic questioner" (Russell Blake, correspondence with the author, Feb. 22, 1995). Further, we must not slight unconventional, experimental modes in favor of more conventional, safe approaches to our craft, such as the lecture mode. Duquesne University, for example, attempts to nurture the spirit of pedagogical adventure through its Hunkele Creative Teaching Awards (Frayer, 1995), given to faculty who not only "set very high standards for their students in mastery of course content" but who also find ways to "assure that other skills such as leadership, critical thinking, analysis, decision making, and problem solving are developed as well" (p. 2).

Fund Classroom Research. Part of scholarship's prestige, charisma, and allure comes from the fact that financial support, financial rewards, and career advancement often accrue from its practice. Headline-catching grants have more often involved research than pedagogy. Thus, incentive has perennially

resided in the corner of research rather than teaching. One of the most prag-
matic, and potentially productive, ways of honoring teaching is to create funds
and grants aimed specifically at supporting, encouraging, and fostering classroom research. Further, when such grants are awarded, they should be widely
publicized in the high style accorded scholarship awards.

Honor Programs and Units. One of the most promising recent trends is
the honoring of programs, groups, and academic units for outstanding pedagogical and curricular achievements. Wergin (1993) points out that "at least a
half-dozen major universities in 1992–93 alone inaugurated departmental
teaching awards" (p. 24).

Considering the mission-driven emphasis upon collaboration and cooperation in the liberal arts institution, the institutional aim should be to make
the honoring of collective units even more commonplace. Particularly exciting
is the prospect of interdisciplinary and interdivisional awards given for the
most innovative achievements in cross-disciplinary teaching and curricular
design, such as interdisciplinary seminars for first-year students, collegewide
senior seminars and capstone courses. Awards of this type would nurture and
promote innovation, interdisciplinary collaboration, departmental and inter-
departmental cooperation, and a collegewide teaching culture, while simulta-
neously moving away from the competitive "star" system associated with
individual awards.

Provide Opportunities for Sharing Expertise. To seek counsel from
colleagues is to honor them. To provide opportunities for exemplary teachers
to share their gifts with colleagues is to recognize their extraordinary level of
achievement in the sophisticated craft of teaching. Realizing the importance of
this sharing, some institutions make a potential awardee's willingness to share
her or his expertise an award criterion. At the University of Georgia (Athens),
one of the selection criteria for the prestigious Josiah Meigs Awards for Excellence in Teaching is the nominee's "willingness to share his/her ideas about
teaching with other teachers through publications, talks, or training of other
faculty or graduate students" (University of Georgia, n.d., p. 2).

Create Innovative Alternative Paradigms. What might be needed most
in the arena of teaching recognition and rewards is a good dash of creativity
and innovation. The conventional teaching award seems a bit worn and frayed
at the edges, and the time seems right to take risks and explore new territory.
While the following list of possibilities is merely illustrative and consists primarily of practices already in place at some institutions, these practices are still
infrequent enough to deserve mention.

Award Certificates of Excellence. Smith and Walvoord (1993) argue
that the standard award paradigm is ineffective, and they "recommend a shift
to . . . the 'certificate' paradigm." The certificate approach is particularly attrac-
tive because it "is not competitive but [instead] is given to all who meet certain explicit criteria that demonstrate excellence" (p. 3; see also Chapter Three).

Establish Endowed Chairs. Although the concept of the endowed chair
for teaching professorships is not new (Edgerton, 1993), in practice it seems

still to be the exception rather than the rule. Certainly more endowed chairs appear to be given for scholarship than for pedagogy. Miami-Dade Community College's strong program of endowed teaching chairs, in which faculty occupy the chairs for a "defined period . . . during which they receive a healthy salary supplement and institutional support to pursue instructional issues of interest" (Weimer, 1990, p.142), is a model that might serve as a potent antidote to the current dearth of endowed chairs for exemplary teaching.

Create Student-Sponsored Awards. Students must be made more central to the process of honoring exemplary teaching. This system seems to have worked well for Cardinal Stritch College, which has a student-initiated and -administered Educator of the Year Award. The selection committee is made up of five to twelve student volunteers, who screen the nominations, determine award recipients, and offer honorariums provided by the student government association (Barbara Reynolds, correspondence with the author, Feb. 28, 1995). At Ripon College, the faculty member chosen by annual ballot of the senior class receives the Senior Award (R. Blake, correspondence with the author, Feb. 22, 1995).

Set Up Special Exhibits of Books and Articles. While many institutions feature displays of faculty scholarship, few boast exhibits of outstanding pedagogical and curricular achievements. Such exhibits would contain publications resulting from classroom research, model syllabi, classroom exercises, and the like. Further, a well-traveled hallway in a classroom building might be designated the Teaching Hall of Fame, its walls hung with portraits of outstanding teachers and a plaque containing the names of all instructors receiving outstanding teaching awards.

Nurture an Institutional Teaching Culture. Perhaps the most potent method of honoring outstanding teaching, and by far the surest way of nurturing it, is to create a rich teaching climate, replete with strong "support and incentive systems for faculty" (Grasha, 1977, p. 47). While achieving this climate is not an easy matter in any institution, the relatively small size and compactness of most liberal arts colleges give them a decided edge over their larger kin in creating fertile collegewide teaching cultures.

An institution's chief academic officers are key to creating a productive teaching culture. They must provide both financial and strongly articulated moral support for programs and activities that nurture a strong teaching environment. Their support might take the form of a center for instructional development, a release-time program to encourage the development of instructional innovations, a travel budget for teaching enhancement activities, and subscriptions to teaching journals. Larger collegewide initiatives might include broadening definitions of scholarship to include classroom research, modifying criteria for sabbatical and leave programs so that leaves for pedagogic improvement are as readily granted as those for discipline-specific research, and instituting small grants programs for instructional development. While some of these endeavors may be both costly and time consuming, other effective practices are neither expensive nor grand in scale. Something as small as a congratulatory or commendatory note to a teacher from the president, dean, or academic chair can serve to motivate and energize as much as any honorarium—in some cases, even more. Above all, academic administrators should make certain that institutional statements about the centrality of teaching are not mere lip service, especially when tenure and promotion applications are reviewed.

Conclusion

The liberal arts institution, because its primary mission is to offer quality instruction to undergraduate students, must strive mightily to honor outstanding teaching. Most importantly, it must do so in a manner that fosters collegiality, community, collaboration, and cooperation, qualities central to its primary mission. Because of the liberal arts college's relatively small size and uncomplicated governance system, its potential for creating holistic programs with institutionwide impact is substantially greater than that of larger research schools.

In a thought-provoking essay on liberal arts for the twenty-first century, M. Garrett Bauman (1987) urges us to realize that "liberal arts is the stuff of time, not stasis" and that "we cannot make ideas run the gauntlet of centuries before admitting them to academia" (p. 39). At this crucial juncture in U.S. higher education, when we can as readily go forward with a fresh and reinvigorated reward paradigm honoring teaching as we can maintain the less than satisfactory status quo, we must recognize the urgency of developing inventive, creative, and nurturing means of honoring teaching. Organizational development of this type is also the stuff of time, not stasis. If Shakespeare's Brutus was right about there being "a tide" in our affairs, "which taken at the flood, leads on to fortune" but if omitted binds us "in shallows and in miseries," then let us catch the current tide of opportunity and ensure ourselves an auspicious voyage.

References

Bauman, M. G. "Liberal Arts for the Twenty-First Century." *Journal of Higher Education*, 1987, *58* (1), 38–45.

Bentley College. *Faculty Manual*. Appendix J. Waltham, Mass.: Bentley College, Sept. 20, 1994.

Bevan, J. M. "It Pays to Reward Good Teachers." *AGB Reports*, 1981, *23* (2), 8–14.

Centra, J. A. *Faculty Development Practices in U.S. Colleges and Universities*. Princeton, N.J.: Educational Testing Service, 1976.

Eble, K. E. *The Aims of College Teaching*. San Francisco: Jossey-Bass, 1983.

Edgerton, R. "The Re-Examination of Faculty Priorities." *Change*, 1993, *25* (4), 10–25.

Frayer, D. (ed.). "Crist, Fleming, Manner and Newton Win Creative Teaching Awards." *Teaching at Duquesne*, 1995, *6* (2), 1–2.

Grasha, A. F. "Faculty Development in the Context of Organizational, Interpersonal, and Personal Constraints." *California Journal of Teacher Education*, 1977, *4* (1), 41–55.

Office of Faculty and Program Development, Boston University Metropolitan College. Boston University, n.d.

Smith, H., and Walvoord, B. "Certifying Teaching Excellence: An Alternative Paradigm to the Teaching Award." *AAHE Bulletin*, 1993, *46* (2), 3–5, 12.

University of Georgia. "The Josiah Meigs Awards for Excellence in Teaching." Brochure. Athens: University of Georgia, n.d.

Wergin, J. "Departmental Awards." *Change,* 1993, 25 (4), 24.

Weimer, M. *Improving College Teaching: Strategies for Developing Instructional Effectiveness.* San Francisco: Jossey-Bass, 1990.

Zahorski, K. J. *St. Norbert College Office of Faculty Development Ninth Annual Report: 1993–94.* De Pere, Wis.: St. Norbert College Press, 1994.

KENNETH J. ZAHORSKI is *professor of English and director of faculty development at St. Norbert College, De Pere, Wisconsin.*

One institution's attempt to review teaching at the departmental
level reflects upon the argument that honoring teaching is best done
departmentally due to disciplinary differences in norms and standards.

Decentralized/Departmental Reward Systems

Joyce Povlacs Lunde, Leverne A. Barrett

During the late 1980s at the University of Nebraska, Lincoln (UNL), a group of faculty from the colleges of agriculture and arts and sciences and instructional consultants from the UNL Teaching and Learning Center were looking for ways to raise the importance of teaching and learning. Opinions among those of us in the group varied about how to bring about changes. Some individuals wanted to focus on "building a teaching community" of individual teachers working across disciplines and colleges who would be inspired to improve teaching. Others wanted the higher levels of administration, such as deans and vice chancellors, to rally the troops to the cause and provide resources to reward motivators. The most enlightening moments came, however, when we in the group realized that the locus of activity to improve the climate for teaching had to be the academic departments.

For most faculty members, the department is their "academic home." For its members, a department is the discipline made manifest, the place where followers are recruited and where collegiality is nurtured. One reason given to justify the existence of academic departments is that they "provide an understandable and workable status system within which the faculty member can be oriented and professionally evaluated" (Andersen, 1977, quoted in Creswell and others, 1990, pp. 8–9). In short, although we may not have fully appreciated it at first, locating the center of change within departments in order to improve the reward structure for teaching made excellent sense.

This chapter describes how reward structures in departments at UNL were altered to give more weight to—and thus to honor—effective teaching. It tells how we got started; describes process and outcomes; and concludes with observations about the department's role in defining and rewarding exemplary teaching.

How We Started: From Universitywide to Departmental Focus

In a preliminary proposal to the Fund for the Improvement of Postsecondary Education (FIPSE), we stated our purpose as the need "to define, encourage, recognize, and reward effective teaching." At that time, there was a sparsity of explicit ways to document and reward effective teaching (Millman, 1981; Seldin, 1984; Miller, 1987). Also, at that time, we believed that undergraduate education would be improved if we could precisely identify ways that teaching activity might be better documented, so that effective teaching might be better rewarded and faculty members thus motivated to improve instruction in their classrooms. The focus of what became known as the Rewarding Teaching project at Nebraska was clarified in a series of proposals to FIPSE, which eventually funded a three-year project (1989–1992) and followed that funding with a national dissemination grant (through 1996).

Project leaders initiated change in incremental steps, starting with four departments—English, psychology, agricultural education, and agronomy—and adding larger groups of new departments each year. As a result of intense activity over four years (three FIPSE, one local), forty of the approximately sixty-six UNL departments that offer undergraduate instruction developed plans to reward teaching (Barrett and others, 1992, 1993). In addition, through the dissemination project, Mutual Encouragement, nineteen other universities have sent representatives to the project's national conferences. Another national project, Peer Review of Teaching, sponsored by the American Association for Higher Education (AAHE) (Hutchings, 1994), includes four UNL units: the departments of mathematics, English, and psychology, and the school of music. A study conducted during the Rewarding Teaching project was able to demonstrate that, in general, faculty in participating departments became more positive about the system for rewarding effective teaching (Lunde and Barrett, 1994).

Working Across Departmental Lines

During the Rewarding Teaching project, departments did not work in isolation from each other, their colleges, and the institution. Strategies for change prescribed activity that occurred across the campus as well as within departments. Top administrators, such as the deans in the colleges where the project originated, were strong advocates for rebuilding reward systems to promote the rewarding of effective teaching. Departmental teams, usually consisting of the chair or head, a member of the promotion and tenure committee, and a senior faculty member designated as the "FIPSE coordinator," met with other teams, project leaders, and administrators. Teams also participated in frequent universitywide meetings and celebrations and had opportunities to attend one or more national conferences on teaching together ideas and plan strategies.

Process to Change the Reward System

Change in the way departments rewarded teaching came about by means of a structured process, with designated players engaging in a sequence of activities that involved as many of the members as possible and that occurred within a stated time frame. Bolstered with resources and encouragement, departmental teams planned and facilitated a year-long series of activities, such as presentations at faculty meetings, retreats, dinner meetings, discussion groups, and work groups, to stimulate thinking and action in their home departments (Wright, 1992).

Departments were encouraged to produce plans "reflective of the values related to teaching, the implications of the kinds of subject matter being taught, the modes of teaching being used (lecture, laboratory, recitation, clinical, etc.), the range of data faculty find acceptable, and the options that can be provided for variable contributions to the teaching mission of the department" (Wright, 1992, p. 9). This encouragement was liberating, but in practice, many of the resulting departmental plans reflect general definitions of effective teaching, standard kinds of evidence, and much overlapping in language and approach.

Departmental Plans: Evidence of Effective Teaching

Departments were the primary arenas for determining what constituted effective teaching and how that teaching would be documented and evaluated. In most departmental plans (Barrett and others, 1993), sources of data to evaluate teaching go well beyond the standard student evaluations of instruction. Most departments in the Rewarding Teaching project (including those at other institutions) employ some version of portfolio evaluation (see, for example, Chapter Nine in this volume; Seldin, 1994; O'Neil and Wright, 1994). Categories of documentation include, in addition to student evaluations, such elements as syllabi, course improvement activities, results of classroom observation, teaching goals and objectives, contributions to teaching, professional development, and teaching publications. In many cases, the use of student evaluations of instruction has been augmented, with the faculty member's statement of analysis, diagnosis, and plans for improvement accompanying the report of his or her student ratings. The method of review is also similar across departments. On an annual basis, in most departments, members of an executive, teaching, or promotion-tenure committee review colleagues' submissions, give feedback, and make recommendations for rewards for both nontenured and tenured faculty.

Expanding Ways to Reward Effective Teaching

Rewards for effective teaching are tied to what each department values: promotion, tenure, merit pay, teaching awards, and access to resources. While rewards for teaching through granting tenure, promotion, and merit pay may seem commonplace to other institution types, departments at research universities that make a major place for teaching in the reward structure are far from common. Ways and means of rewarding outstanding teaching are illustrated below.

Promotion, Tenure, and Merit Pay. With multiple documentation of the nature and quality of teaching activity now available, departments can propose a system of quantitative measures for these activities. For instance, the department of psychology at UNL has an extensive list of items that may be submitted in the annual review in addition to the required items of student evaluations and course syllabi. The department executive committee rates the information on teaching and weights it "in a formal mathematical evaluation system that includes research and service along with teaching." The members of this department believe that "building evaluation of teaching into the fabric of the department's personnel processes guarantees that teaching will have importance comparable to that of research and other scholarly activities" (Daniel J. Bernstein, written communication to the authors, 1995).

Increasing Nominations for Teaching Awards. Some departments have rediscovered distinguished teaching awards. At the University of Nebraska, participation in the Rewarding Teaching project alerted departments that previously had not competed to the potential for university awards. Although seeking such awards takes a fair amount of collective effort, over time the pay-off can be greater than at first might be thought possible. Even if a nomination does not produce a public reward, the act of being nominated by one's department is gratifying in itself.

Faculty Development Leaves for Teaching. It has long been assumed that sabbatical leaves at research universities will be used to improve faculty members' records in research and publication in their disciplines. Faculty development leaves for teaching enhancement, however, are becoming possible. In departments in the UNL College of Agriculture, for example, faculty development leaves for teaching are encouraged when the greater proportion of the assignment lies in teaching.

Special Resources. Effective teaching can be rewarded by providing funds for other material resources and travel beyond usual funding. Access to funds for purchasing such items as computer upgrades, scholarly books, CD-ROMs, videotaped materials, and specialized laboratory equipment are some examples. Other rewards where merit pay is scarce have included reserved parking spaces, theater tickets, and other nonmonetary perks. In the University of Cincinnati Department of Economics, motivation and reward for teaching might come in the form of favorable teaching assignments or schedules. An annual departmental dinner and a teaching award offered by the undergraduate economics majors also provide opportunities for recognition (Philip K. Wey, written communication to the authors, 1995).

Institutional Rewards. The institution itself can encourage departments to recognize and reward effective teaching. In the early stages of the Rewarding Teaching project, the dean of arts and sciences at UNL increased merit pay funds for those departments that had written plans in place to reward teaching. Another way to honor teaching is to reward an entire department. An annual award established by the University of Nebraska within its four-campus system offers $25,000 to the department whose members can collectively demonstrate excellence in teaching. In 1994, the award went to the UNL English department, which is now using these funds for special teaching-related grants and awards.

Departmental Reward Systems and the Discipline

At Nebraska, the focus on improving the reward system via promotion, tenure, and merit pay gave faculty a common goal and framework from the start but perhaps constrained the development of different approaches to rewarding effective teaching. In many cases, departments studied the plans of others before coming up with their own. Geography, for example, acknowledges its debt to music (Barrett and others, 1993, p. L12).

Differences in criteria can be based on what the department values. Applied disciplines, for instance, connect criteria for outstanding teaching with career preparation. In their "philosophy," Department of Food Science and Technology faculty "are committed to have a strong scholastic program for the training of the future generation(s) of leaders in the food industry" and are encouraged to have the "latest knowledge available" to present to their students (Barrett and others, 1993, p. J1).

The UNL School of Music sets forth separate lists of "Criteria of Excellence in Teaching" for studio, ensemble, and classroom teaching. For example, one criterion reads: "A good studio teacher is fully acquainted with traditional literature, performance styles and techniques, and interpretations, and keeps up with current development in these areas, as well as trends in equipment and instruments and other relevant technology, and communicates this information to students" (Barrett and others, 1993, p. Q4.).

Conclusion

There is no one-dimensional answer to how teaching can be elevated and honored in a given department on a given university campus. The catalyst, expertise, and energy for putting a recognition system in place may originate from outside of the department. However, if the department truly has the will to recognize and reward outstanding teaching, it not only invites in external resources but it also works collectively within its membership and its discipline to build, promote, and maintain a reward system of its own.

References

Andersen, K. J. "In Defense of Departments." In D. E. McHenry and Associates, *Academic Departments*. San Francisco: Jossey-Bass, 1977. Quoted in J. W. Creswell, D. W. Wheeler,

A. T. Seagren, N. J. Egly, and K. D. Beyer, *The Academic Chairperson's Handbook.* Lincoln: University of Nebraska Press, 1990.

Barrett, L. A., Narveson, R. D., Wright, D. L., Bernstein, D. J., and Burkholder, A. G. *From Regard to Reward: Improving Teaching at a Research-Oriented University: The Final Report.* Fund for the Improvement of Postsecondary Education grant number P1161391612–90. Lincoln: University of Nebraska, Lincoln, Teaching and Learning Center, 1992.

Barrett, L. A., Narveson, R. D., Wright, D. L., Bernstein, D. J., and Burkholder, A. G. *From Regard to Reward: Improving Teaching at a Research-Oriented University. Department Plans: Documentation, Evaluation, Reward.* Lincoln: University of Nebraska, Lincoln, Teaching and Learning Center, 1993.

Hutchings, P. "Peer Review of Teaching: From Idea to Prototype." *AAHE Bulletin,* 1994, 47 (3), 3–7.

Lunde, J. P., and Barrett, L. A. "Impact of an Intervention to Improve the Rewards for Teaching at a Research-Oriented University." Paper presented at the Annual Conference of the American Educational Research Association, New Orleans, Apr. 5, 1994. (ED 372 667 RIEDEC94)

Miller, R. I. *Evaluating Faculty for Promotion and Tenure.* San Francisco: Jossey-Bass, 1987.

Millman, J. (ed.). *Handbook of Teacher Evaluation.* Newbury Park, Calif.: Sage, 1981.

O'Neil, C., and Wright, A. *Recording Teaching Accomplishment: A Dalhousie Guide to the Teaching Dossier.* (4th ed.) Halifax, Nova Scotia: Dalhousie University, 1994.

Seldin, P. *Changing Practices in Faculty Evaluation: A Critical Assessment and Recommendations for Improvement.* San Francisco: Jossey-Bass, 1984.

Seldin, P. *Successful Use of Teaching Portfolios.* Bolton, Mass.: Anker, 1994.

Study Group on the Conditions of Excellence in American Higher Education. *Involvement in Learning: Realizing the Potential of American Higher Education.* Washington, D.C.: National Institute of Education, 1984.

Wright, D. L. *From Regard to Reward. How to Proceed: Department to College to Institution.* Lincoln: University of Nebraska, Lincoln, Teaching and Learning Center, 1992.

JOYCE POVLACS LUNDE *is associate professor of agricultural leadership, education, and communication at University of Nebraska, Lincoln.*

LEVERNE A. BARRETT *is professor of agricultural leadership, education, and communication at University of Nebraska, Lincoln.*

Because military academies approach higher education from a special perspective and faculty are mostly military officers with special experiences of evaluation, they approach honoring teaching somewhat differently from other institutions.

Promoting Exemplary Teaching: The Case of the U.S. Military Academy

George B. Forsythe, Anita Gandolfo

Several years ago, one of our departments had difficulty recruiting a faculty member to spend the year doing full-time fully funded research. The reason for this difficulty may seem unusual to anyone familiar with the current crisis in undergraduate teaching. So valued is the teaching enterprise in the department that, despite the fact that the department had many highly qualified research scholars, we could not find anyone willing to accept the research position because no one wanted to give up all teaching responsibilities.

We share this story to highlight our belief that developing reward programs as a means of improving undergraduate teaching should be viewed with caution. Central to the issue of instructional improvement must be the understanding that no awards program will be effective in promoting exemplary teaching if teaching and learning are not valued in the institutional culture. Where they are, perhaps awards programs are unnecessary or irrelevant for celebrating teaching excellence.

In this chapter, we present the case of the United States Military Academy (USMA), an institution where undergraduate teaching is the valued enterprise. We examine the internal debate over teaching awards within this specific academic culture and explore alternatives for celebrating exemplary teaching.

Note: The views and opinions expressed herein are solely those of the authors and do not represent the official view of the U.S. Military Academy, the U.S. Army, or any other agency of the U.S. Government.

Teaching at USMA

To better understand the context for teaching at USMA, it is helpful to know that our 4,000 undergraduate students are enrolled in a four-year baccalaureate program that is augmented with rigorous military, physical, and leadership training. Seventy percent of the academic curriculum is in common "core" courses in the humanities, sciences, and engineering, while 30 percent of the curriculum provides more depth of study. The Academy's teaching enterprise has been shaped by the "Thayer System" (named for the superintendent of the academy from 1817 to 1833, who established its basic system of instruction, patterned after European universities he visited). This system emphasizes small class sections (fifteen to eighteen students), daily recitations, frequent evaluations, and attention to the development of the whole person. At USMA, education is not an end in itself but the means to the larger end of leader development. At the present time, 65 percent of our faculty are from the field Army, coming from graduate school (usually upon completion of a master's degree) for a three-year faculty appointment. The remaining 35 percent are military and civilian faculty with the Ph.D. degree, most of whom hold appointments for longer periods of time. The senior military faculty are principally responsible for curriculum and faculty development. They observe classroom teaching and serve as mentors for junior faculty. The principal assignment of the junior faculty is teaching, but all have additional duties in support of instruction: for example, as audiovisual liaisons, computer assistants, and members of core course instructional "teams" who take responsibility for individual segments of the course. Much of our teaching (and all of the teaching in core curriculum courses) is accomplished by such faculty teams.

Since faculty turnover is high (approximately 25 percent annually), faculty development is a continuous process at USMA. However, our development efforts are conducted within the framework of the fact that the largest percentage of USMA faculty are Army leaders, who are experienced with individual and group learning in an occupational training context. As leaders, they present the following profile:

They bring to the teaching role a value that the leader is responsible for everything the unit does or fails to do. This means they will take the teaching task seriously and may assume some of the responsibility to ensure that the students "learn."

They have experience in the teaching-learning process but less experience in intellectual growth and development.

Their professional self-concept is tied more to the military profession than to the discipline in which they teach. They seek an assignment at USMA to "pass on the [military] profession," not to make cadets better psychologists, poets, or engineers.

Teaching Awards

From 1977 to 1987, USMA had one institutional-level award for teaching excellence. This award had been provided to the academy by an outside bene-factor, to honor the person in whose name the award was given. (The other service academies have similar awards.) There was a lack of consensus on the criteria for the award and the value of the award to the faculty. In practice, the award seemed to be passed among departments, with "teaching excellence" determined by whose turn it was to receive recognition. USMA finally canceled the program in 1987 as a result of faculty feeling that the award was mean-ingless and divisive.

However, in 1988, as a result of the decennial reaccreditation self-study, the faculty recommended that the dean (chief academic officer at USMA) take steps to increase institutional emphasis on the evaluation of instruction and to provide greater recognition for excellence in teaching. The dean subsequently charged the Teaching Excellence Committee of the faculty council with explor-ing the issue of recognition of teaching excellence, and the committee con-ducted a survey of the faculty to assess the level of interest in teaching awards. The results of that survey indicated that there was moderate consensus (58 per-cent) in favor of awards, with considerable ambivalence on the part of the senior faculty; no consensus on program level (centralized USMA awards or decentralized departmental awards), although the strongest support was for departmental awards; support for award criteria that would include excellent and/or creative teaching and other scholarship but no support for such crite-ria as involvement in cadet extracurricular activities or community service; and support for supervisor and student input on awards but no specification of the details of administering awards.

The solution was to use an existing program sponsored by the local Phi Kappa Phi Honor Society. Under this program, departments would be respon-sible for their own criteria for the award and for the nomination of one or two faculty members. A certificate and a $50 savings bond would be awarded to the departmental nominees. The faculty decided to pilot this concept for a year and reevaluate the program.

The subsequent evaluation indicated problems. Departments used the award in different ways, most of which were unrelated to exemplary teaching. Faculty remained divided on the issue of continuing the program. There was a feeling that the academy had not sufficiently articulated criteria for assessing exemplary teaching, and there was a fear that this program would promote divisiveness. The dean asked the Teaching Excellence Committee to revisit the issue of recognition for teaching excellence and specifically to consider how other institutions promote good teaching.

However, this investigation also highlighted the ways in which good teach-ing is currently acknowledged at USMA. Outstanding teaching is promoted and celebrated through holding departmental conferences and workshops on teaching, asking exemplary faculty to conduct workshops for their peers, and/or giving excellent teachers among the rotating faculty the more prestigious assignments in advanced electives.

There is also a system of reward in place for the military faculty. A military officer's performance is reviewed annually, and that report is crucial to a person's selection for command or further schooling. Hence, for officers assigned to USMA, evaluation of their teaching is crucial to their career advancement, perhaps more crucial than for faculty in civilian institutions. Thus, the faculty request for some standardized criteria for teaching excellence was very likely a reflection of the fact that the academy has a responsibility to ensure that evaluations are properly measuring teaching effectiveness rather than tangential aspects of faculty citizenship, such as cooperation or congeniality.

Continuing Issues

The academy still struggles with the self-study conclusion that it needs to acknowledge teaching more directly. Many issues have surfaced from the continued discussion of teaching rewards.

There is general agreement that teaching awards have a three-fold purpose: to motivate and encourage attention to the teaching role, to model exemplary teaching, and to improve student learning. Less clear is whether an award system would accomplish these purposes. If we want to experiment once again with an award system, do we opt for one academy-level award or several awards? And if we choose to have more than one, just how many would be appropriate? In addition, there is the question of how criteria will be established. If there are to be USMA awards, should criteria be institution specific or are there substantive differences among disciplines that warrant separate sets of criteria? Should we have a centralized nomination and selection process or must the program be fully decentralized?

The problem, of course, is that there is less quality control in a decentralized program. Our experience with the Phi Kappa Phi award is illustrative. Departments used the award in various ways, many of which were unrelated to excellence in teaching. Even with renewed emphasis on an award for teaching excellence, the question of criteria for the award is coupled with the issue of administration; more specifically, who provides input? Although some departments currently use peer and student input, the tendency is to make judgments based on evaluation by senior experienced faculty, as is customary in the military performance evaluation system. Given the strong hierarchical structure of the Army, a teaching award that is based on information from multiple sources might be viewed as having less rigorous standards and, therefore, as less prestigious.

In addition, there is some concern that an award program might exacerbate what is already a highly competitive system of professional advancement for Army officers who are not career academics. This concern is understandable in light of the academy's corporate culture, which promotes collaboration among faculty working in teaching teams. There is thus a tendency not to make excellence in teaching public but to limit acknowledgment of that excellence to the annual performance report, which, as noted earlier, is the crucial document for career advancement in the military. This model might also serve the increased number of civilian faculty better than an award system. That is, an annual evaluation of teaching that regularly cites excellence according to department-specific criteria may be a better indicator of potential for academic promotion than receiving a single award for teaching excellence.

Celebrating Rather Than Rewarding Teaching

If a teaching awards program becomes the test case for an institution's dedication to teaching excellence, programs may proliferate with no relation to exemplary teaching. The U.S. Military Academy claims a reputation for academic excellence, yet does not have a substantial teaching awards program. Why? There are several possible explanations, some of which indicate how this situation can be misinterpreted.

For example, is our concern for teaching more rhetoric than reality? This is unlikely. Both the cadets and external accrediting bodies say we do a good job in teaching. A more likely explanation is that exemplary teaching is considered the military faculty member's duty, and the rating on the annual performance evaluation report is the most potent "award" in that culture.

While there is universal agreement on the primacy of teaching at USMA, there is no consensus on the means. Faculty insist on discipline-specific criteria for measuring teaching effectiveness, and this argues against a centralized awards program.

Finally, while we do recognize good teaching that recognition manifests itself in forms different from those at other institutions. For Army officers assigned to USMA, as noted above, the importance of teaching is taken for granted, and excellence is rewarded within the military culture. In the military, there is a tendency not to go outside the normal award systems to acknowledge individual performance, and this practice carries over to the faculty role at the academy. It is in this context that the faculty charge to the dean in the 1988 self-study should be understood. The request to "increase emphasis on the evaluation of instruction and to provide greater recognition for excellence in teaching" can be understood as a request for a greater focus on the academy's principal mission, by helping USMA faculty understand how best to perform the job to which they are committed.

In 1994, USMA inaugurated its Center for Teaching Excellence (CTE), and that unit is perhaps the best answer to the 1988 request. The emphasis of the center is sharing and celebrating the high-quality teaching of the faculty rather than rewarding it.

The CTE has two major functions: to provide opportunities for faculty members to develop and extend their skills and competencies, and to exert leadership in helping the faculty identify and establish standards of excellence in teaching. It is hoped that the much sought criteria for teaching excellence will evolve as USMA faculty become increasingly engaged in quality conversations about teaching and learning. To celebrate exemplary teaching, plans for the future include the inauguration of *Teaching Abstracts*, a local publication of successful teaching innovations and lessons learned from research in the Advanced Technology Classroom/Laboratory, and teaching fellowships, stipends to support faculty research in instructional development and improvement of learning outcomes.

The CTE is also exploring ways to link faculty development projects (for example, the compiling of teaching portfolios) to a centralized teaching excellence recognition program. The lesson of the past several years is clear. If USMA is to recognize exemplary teaching at the institutional as well as at the departmental level, the process must develop through consensus of major stakeholders.

Conclusion

It is apparent from the USMA experience that the rewarding of excellent teaching is not a unilateral issue but one that must emanate from a particular teaching culture. Academy faculty reluctance to embrace a centralized award program is not a sign that teaching lacks value but a recognition of the pitfalls of adopting a model that might be excellent for a very different institution but not a good fit with our institutional culture. Rewarding exemplary teaching at USMA is a process that has evolved in an exclusively military environment but must now adapt to our increasing number of civilian faculty.

We believe that the academy experience is instructive. Not only must any program for rewarding exemplary teaching be institution specific, it must also be responsive to the institution's evolving nature. At USMA, we pride ourselves on a tradition of excellence in teaching, while, at the same time, continually learning what excellence in teaching means at the present moment in our history.

GEORGE B. FORSYTHE is professor of psychology and leadership and associate dean for academic affairs at the United States Military Academy.

ANITA GANDOLFO is professor of English and director of the Center for Teaching Excellence at the United States Military Academy.

Can disciplinary societies take the lead in honoring exemplary teaching? One organization is proposing a process to do just that.

Promoting Excellence in Teaching in Pharmaceutical Education: The Master Teacher Credentialling Program

Susan M. Meyer, Richard P. Penna

The American Association of Colleges of Pharmacy is the national professional society representing pharmaceutical education in the United States. The association membership is composed of each of the U.S. schools and colleges of pharmacy and approximately 2,200 faculty members. Moreover, all nine Canadian faculties of pharmacy as well as many from such other countries as the Philippines, Malaysia, Thailand, and Wales hold affiliate membership in the association.

Within its Center for the Advancement of Pharmaceutical Education, the association is developing a program that will identify and/or create resources and programs to assist faculty members to improve their teaching skills; identify and/or create assessment tools so that faculty may evaluate their own and peer teaching skills; assemble a national board to develop criteria for determining teaching excellence; and institute a credentialling, or certification, system for the designation Master Teacher in Pharmaceutical Education.

The Need

It has been said that teaching is currency without value across universities, schools, and colleges (Boyer, 1990). Research excellence is understood within a discipline across institutions, but teaching excellence is not. Pharmaceutical education or any health-profession education needs such a "national currency" of criteria and standards of teaching excellence, validated by a national recognition system for faculty who meet these criteria, as does higher education in general. The Master Teacher program will provide needed information about the operations, process, acceptability, and outcomes of certifying teaching excellence within pharmaceutical education on which to base this "currency."

Pharmaceutical education is undergoing major organizational and curricular changes in order to meet the educational needs of students and practitioners. A Commission to Implement Change in Pharmaceutical Education, appointed by the association, prepared a mission statement for pharmaceutical education and issued a background paper (Penna, 1994) outlining the educational outcomes and process of a revised pharmaceutical professional curriculum to prepare practitioners to serve society's needs in a reformed health care system. As a result of the commission's work, the faculties of most U.S. schools and colleges of pharmacy are undertaking profound curricular evaluation and restructuring to meet the competencies outlined by the statement. As a result of these efforts, a number of teaching needs have been identified. Practitioners will need to be recruited as part-time faculty to teach in the experiential portions of the curriculum; these practitioners will need to be developed as educators (that is, taught the appropriate skills); the teaching skills of all faculty and their facility with different instructional and assessment methods need to be improved; and, finally, stimulating and promoting excellence in teaching among all pharmacy faculty will need to be a priority.

Support Within and Outside of Pharmaceutical Education

There is long-standing and universal support both within and outside of pharmaceutical education for resources that would help teachers assess, improve, and develop their own teaching skills. Discussion related to the recognizing or credentialling of excellence in teaching by a national body is a more recent development.

In 1992, the association's Academic Affairs Committee discussed the evaluation and rewarding of excellence in teaching and service (Vanderveen, 1992). The committee identified the need to develop a master teacher credential for pharmacy school faculty, and it recommended that "AACP should consider the development and implementation of a program to both recognize Master Teachers at the national level and provide opportunities for skill development to assist those faculty who seek to improve their teaching effectiveness."

The committee went on to suggest:

The Master Teacher program could highlight innovations in teaching in pharmaceutical education: basic science, pharmaceutical science, clinical science, and practice.

The Master Teacher program should be a high level, rigorous program to recognize effective teachers as well as provide opportunities for . . . those who seek to improve . . . and who aspire to Master Teacher status. The program could be coordinated by AACP and structured as a certificate or curricular-based program in teaching skills and strategies. [Vanderveen, 1992, p. 8S]

The Program

In July 1993, AACP established the Center for the Advancement of Pharmaceutical Education (CAPE). The center was to develop resources and programs to assist faculty members in improving their teaching skills, to develop assessment tools to evaluate teaching skills, to develop criteria for determining excellence in teaching, and to establish a credentialling system to recognize faculty members who meet the established criteria and demonstrate excellence in teaching.

The advisory panel on the Master Teacher was appointed, and that panel determined that the Master Teacher designation should be a credential awarded to faculty of schools and colleges of pharmacy who provide evidence that their teaching meets or exceeds pertinent standards or criteria. The program will be available to full-time, university-based faculty and part-time, field-based practitioner faculty. The credentialling process will comply with the following description. It will be objective and equitable, reliable and consistent, valid and authentic, legitimate, rigorous, and diagnostic. The credentialling process will discriminate between novice teachers and master teachers. It will assess and acknowledge quality, quantity, and innovation in teaching. The credentialling process will include the following steps:

1. With the assistance of consultants, an extensive search will be undertaken to identify those resources, programs, and assessment tools already in existence (within and outside of pharmaceutical education) that could be used to assess and improve the teaching skills of faculty. Gaps in existing resources, programs, and assessment tools will be identified. The program will request proposals from schools and colleges of pharmacy, working cooperatively with schools and colleges of education to develop those additional resources, programs, and assessment tools that are needed.

2. The program will establish and approve criteria and standards for determining excellence in teaching. Criteria and standards will be developed by the program advisory panel, submitted to member faculty for review and comment, revised as necessary, and submitted to the association's board of directors for adoption. Because the criteria will have been developed with the active participation of pharmacy school faculty, it is expected that the resulting credential will be "currency" that is broadly recognized in pharmaceutical education.

3. A body to evaluate evidence submitted by candidates (National Board of Teaching Excellence in Pharmaceutical Education) will be created.

4. Pharmaceutical educators who wish to be credentialed will submit portfolios to the national board, which will assess evidence and provide diagnostic feedback to candidates.

5. The national board will credential those faculty members whose evidence is judged to meet or exceed the criteria and standards. The credential will remain valid for a limited period of time to be established by the national board.

Feedback to candidates, regardless of the credentialling decision (reject, candidate status, or credentialed) will be diagnostic to foster each candidate's continued development.

Preliminary Criteria and Standards

The CAPE Advisory Panel on the Master Teacher has proposed eleven preliminary criteria for excellence in teaching. Seven are taken from Chickering, Gamson, and Barsi's *Seven Principles of Good Practice in Undergraduate Education* (1987). Good practice encourages student-faculty contact, encourages cooperation among students, encourages active learning, gives prompt feedback, emphasizes time on task, communicates high expectations, and respects diverse talents and ways of learning.

The remaining four preliminary criteria are that content of teaching be current, up-to-date, and sufficient to meet goals of the course(s); candidates participate in and contribute to the scholarly discourse on pharmaceutical education, clinical education, and/or professional education; candidates engage in scholarly inquiry into their own teaching practices; and candidates conduct their practices of teaching within well-reasoned, explicitly articulated philosophical and theoretical frameworks of professional/pharmaceutical education.

Conclusion

The association anticipates that the project will require at least three years to develop and evaluate resources and programs. At the end of that time, we may be able to point to this project as the basis for that "national currency" in teaching toward which we aspire.

References

Boyer, E. L. *Scholarship Reconsidered: Priorities of the Professoriate*. Princeton, N.J.: The Carnegie Foundation for the Advancement of Teaching, 1990.

Chickering, A. W., Gamson, Z. F., and Barsi, L. M. *Seven Principles of Good Practice in Undergraduate Education*. Washington, D.C.: American Association of Higher Education, 1987.

Penna, R. P. (ed.). *The Papers of the Commission to Implement Change in Pharmaceutical Education*. Alexandria, Va.: American Association of Colleges of Pharmacy, 1994.

Vanderveen, R. P. "Chair Report of the Academic Affairs Committee." *American Journal of Pharmaceutical Education*, 1992, 56 (supplement), 8S–12S.

SUSAN M. MEYER *is director of academic affairs, American Association of Colleges of Pharmacy.*

RICHARD P. PENNA *is executive director, American Association of Colleges of Pharmacy.*

A synthesis of suggestions and cautions about establishing recognition programs takes the form of ten guidelines that apply regardless of program format and context.

Consistency Within Diversity: Guidelines for Programs to Honor Exemplary Teaching

Marilla D. Svinicki, Robert J. Menges

Is the climate for teaching in higher education changing? It appears to be, at least here and there and in fits and starts. Many factors have turned the spotlight on teaching. Unfortunately, it has often been the spotlight of criticism or investigation. We hope this volume has put teaching in a different light, a spotlight of praise and celebration. If we have been successful, perhaps the public's attention will be turned not to those who fail the public trust but to those who labor long and hard in the interest of providing an education of quality for their students.

Inside and outside the academy, there nevertheless remains some skepticism about the ways educators identify and reward good teaching. The skeptics' arguments have been adequately reviewed in the preceding chapters and need not be repeated here. However, they do remind us that new programs to identify and reward teaching must be above suspicion if they are to be credible and effective.

This concluding chapter identifies characteristics of good programs that will meet those standards.

Guidelines for Exemplary Programs

Those who design programs to recognize excellence in teaching are more likely to create systems capable of withstanding criticism if they keep the following ten points in mind.

NEW DIRECTIONS FOR TEACHING AND LEARNING, no. 65, Spring 1996 © Jossey-Bass Publishers

1. *The program is consistent with the institution's mission and values, and it communicates those values to the community.* A program to recognize exemplary teaching must be consistent with the mission and values of its institution. Although almost all the institutions described in this volume have teaching as one of their missions, there are as many levels of emphasis as there are institutions. For community colleges and liberal arts colleges, programs to recognize exemplary teaching are almost synonymous with their existence. At comprehensive and research institutions, however, teaching is only one of many components of the institutional mission.

In all cases, the structure of a program to honor exemplary teaching conveys important messages, both inside and outside about the institution's teaching standards. Expressing those standards can help revitalize senior faculty as well as inspire and guide junior faculty and instigates a discussion of values that can invigorate the scholarly life of the academy. When more and more constituencies within the institution take part in this discussion, the definition of teaching will become richer and more representative of the true nature of the academy.

2. *The program is grounded in research-based teaching competencies rather than dependent on special interests, favoritism, or popularity.* Because teaching is difficult to study, some have argued that it cannot be studied. Critics who refuse to study it feel free to fall back on hearsay, personal anecdotes, and questionable survey research.

Fortunately, research about teaching has now attained a level of sophistication that supports stable conclusions and generalizations about what makes for excellence. From the chapters in this volume that discuss the adequacy of different forms of data collection, we can discern a sufficient database to inform our work. While not all exemplary teachers will always display all the characteristics of good teaching all the time, we can be confident enough in the research data to advise looking for a consistent pattern featuring a majority of those characteristics. The pattern will reveal a solid teaching base which, enlivened by inspiration and innovation, may rise to the level of exemplary teaching.

3. *The program recognizes all significant facets of instructional activities that are conducted by the faculty.* For some faculty and other interest groups, teaching is equated with what happens within the walls of the classroom. However, there are many venues in which the interaction between teachers and students contributes as much or more to student development. Some of the best teaching occurs in laboratories, fieldwork settings, or informal interactions, by e-mail or telephone, with student interest groups, and individual consultation.

In addition, many aspects of exemplary teaching may involve no student contact at all—time devoted to the design of course materials, texts, evaluation instruments, and computer-based instructional packages; energy directed toward evaluating students' work and providing feedback; efforts devoted to curriculum committee deliberations about core curricula and requirements. All these and more lay the groundwork for a solid educational foundation on which excellent classroom work can be built. In addition, the best teachers press for institutional change to enhance the students' education.

4. *The program rewards collaborative as well as individual achievements.* The common vision of teaching focuses on the lone instructor surrounded by a group of students, but this is only one model of teaching. There is much to be said for encouraging and recognizing collaborative efforts among faculty. Collaboration offers students a different vision of scholarship. Many disciplines, especially the sciences, have moved more and more toward joint work as projects and programs increase in complexity. Encouraging faculty to work together in teams to teach as well as to do research helps students learn the skills necessary to function in our increasingly collaborative environment.

A second reason for encouraging programs that recognize collaboration is the divisive effect of competition on what should be a collegial enterprise. To imply that only one person can be recognized as "the" exemplary teacher or that exemplary teaching occurs only through the agency of an individual is to support an erroneous view of the academy.

5. *The program neither precludes nor displaces rewards for teaching that are part of the institutionalized reward system.* It is important to remember that recognition of teaching should be an ongoing rather than a one-time experience; it must permeate the institution's reward system. To assume that making a teacher-of-the-year award would satisfy our responsibility to nurture good teaching would be gross negligence.

When rewards for exemplary teaching become part of the institutionalized reward system, they provide a solid base on which to rest the periodic recognition of outstanding teachers. When teaching is one focus of the regular incentive system, faculty become more sensitive to the qualities that make for great teaching when the time comes to recognize faculty who are outstanding.

6. *The program calls on those who have been honored to continue to contribute to the development of others.* Programs that do more than knight an individual as an exemplary teacher are making use of the existing culture of the academy to further the teaching mission. One feature of that culture is that faculty members prefer to learn from one another, rather than an outsider. The role of award-winning faculty as peer models can inspire others and encourage them to reflect on their own teaching. At the same time, those in the spotlight benefit from the requirement to describe and reflect. Through the self-reflection process, they can become even stronger advocates of teaching as they reveal unstated assumptions about practices in which they engage.

Award winners can serve not only as models for all faculty but also as mentors for new faculty and graduate students. Award winners can explain the work of the institution to the outside community as well. While many outside the academy do not understand the world of research and scholarship, they can understand the value of teaching and make a connection with the institution through these individuals who represent the teaching role of the faculty.

It is the authors' experience that award winners find themselves speaking on behalf of the journeyman teachers who have labored long and hard in basic classes. They offer advice on the design of learning spaces. They speak to prospective students. They represent the teaching interests of the academy on policy-making bodies. For many institutions, these interests have not had representation for too long, and this representation makes it possible to include teaching in all sorts of academic and nonacademic decisions. As these individuals speak about the pedagogical implications of institutional decisions, they help legitimize the practice of including pedagogical considerations in all important decision-making processes.

7. *The program contributes to collegial responsibility for promoting exemplary teaching.* Most award programs are based on nomination and selection by educators' peers and by students. An interesting process occurs when faculty are asked to identify persons among their ranks who are worthy of recognition: they begin to examine their own assumptions about what constitutes good teaching. By playing an active role in the selection process and working with others on the task, faculty bring their values about teaching to a conscious level and make a commitment to the criteria and the selection process used to identify exemplary colleagues.

Once criteria for selection are identified, the markers of poor teaching will come into sharper contrast for most faculty. However unconsciously, they will begin to look around and assess all the teaching at the institution. This increased scrutiny can lead to improved practice even among those who are not being considered for an award.

8. *The program encourages self-reflection at all levels of the institution.* Establishing criteria that accompany the honoring of teaching is only the first step. It is a part of the self-reflection that marks self-regulating institutions and individuals. Through reflection, each individual faculty member can determine to what extent his or her behavior is consistent with the criteria identified. Aggregates of faculty, within either a department or a discipline, can discuss the implications for their collective performance of having each individual work toward the criteria. They might also discover that group-level criteria can be derived from individual criteria. For example, if exemplary teachers take care to learn as much about their students as possible, departments wishing to promote this same behavior in their faculty might gather data and create departmental norms that help individual faculty learn about their students. At an institutional level, there might be more sharing of information across departments so that students can move easily from one to another.

Just as exemplary teachers modify their teaching to assist students from diverse backgrounds and learning styles, an institution of exemplary teachers would note where institutional practices are not responsive to that diversity due to outmoded assumptions or bureaucratic artifice. Conversely, programs that recognize exemplary teachers should recognize particular institutional practices that facilitate exemplary teaching, for the teacher should be only one component of a team that functions seamlessly in support of learning.

9. *The program is based on sound assessment practices, including multiple data sources, multiple measures, and consistency over time.* Several of this volume's

authors discuss the importance of defensible selection practices and criteria. Institutions setting up new programs to honor exemplary teaching are advised not to rush into implementation but to consider their procedures carefully. We are no longer dependent on hearsay evidence of teaching. We can apply adequate evaluation methods and be certain that teachers identified as exemplary do indeed fit the definition.

If care is taken from the outset, the program will be able to focus on its primary function—to honor teachers. It is less likely to be drawn into political and interpersonal squabbles about whether or not the selection process is fair and accurate. By building procedures with care, the institution also models appropriate assessment strategies that individuals and departments can use for the more mundane decisions about retention, merit raises, and tenure and promotion.

10. *The program itself is open to scrutiny and change as conditions change.* It would be foolish to think that a program designed with today's academy in mind will be forever applicable and appropriate. The world of higher education changes slowly, but it does change. Practices that were standard even fifty years ago no longer apply to today's diverse institutions. The marks of good teaching may also change as the defining activities of teaching change. Will we be able to apply the same criteria that were developed for the lecture-based classroom to teaching in cyberspace? The very nature of teaching may change; therefore, periodic review and assessment should be part of the program design.

Conclusion

Teaching is a difficult and honorable calling and deserves to be recognized as such. This is the time to bring teaching out of the closet, not in order to condemn those who do poorly, but to honor those who add luster to the calling. If institutions wish to be true to their teaching mission, they must seek out faculty who do the most to exemplify that mission. They must proclaim to all who will listen that it is the teachers who hold the keys to the future—the future for the students, for the institution, for the disciplines, and for higher education itself.

MARILLA D. SVINICKI, associate editor, is director, Center for Teaching Effectiveness, University of Texas, Austin.

ROBERT J. MENGES, editor-in-chief, is professor of education and social policy, Northwestern University, and senior researcher, National Center on Postsecondary Teaching, Learning, and Assessment.

INDEX

ORDERING INFORMATION

NEW DIRECTIONS FOR TEACHING AND LEARNING is a series of paperback books that presents ideas and techniques for improving college teaching, based both on the practical expertise of seasoned instructors and on the latest research findings of educational and psychological researchers. Books in the series are published quarterly in Spring, Summer, Fall, and Winter and are available for purchase by subscription as well as by single copy.

SUBSCRIPTIONS for 1996 cost $50.00 for individuals (a savings of 34 percent over single-copy prices) and $72.00 for institutions, agencies, and libraries. Please do not send institutional checks for personal subscriptions. Standing orders are accepted. (For subscriptions outside of North America, add $7.00 for shipping via surface mail or $25.00 for air mail. Orders *must be prepaid* in U.S. dollars by check drawn on a U.S. bank or charged to VISA, MasterCard, or American Express.)

SINGLE COPIES cost $19.00 plus shipping (see below) when payment accompanies order. California, New Jersey, New York, and Washington, D.C., residents please include appropriate sales tax. Canadian residents add GST and any local taxes. Billed orders will be charged shipping and handling. No billed shipments to post office boxes. (Orders from outside North America *must be prepaid* in U.S. dollars by check drawn on a U.S. bank or charged to VISA, MasterCard, or American Express.)

SHIPPING (SINGLE COPIES ONLY): $10.00 and under, add $2.50; to $20.00, add $3.50; to $50.00, add $4.50; to $75.00, add $5.50; to $100.00, add $6.50; to $150.00, add $7.50; over $150.00, add $8.50.

DISCOUNTS FOR QUANTITY ORDERS are available. Please write to the address below for information.

ALL ORDERS must include either the name of an individual or an official purchase order number. Please submit your order as follows:
    Subscriptions: specify series and year subscription is to begin
    Single copies: include individual title code (such as TL54)

MAIL ALL ORDERS TO:
    Jossey-Bass Publishers
    350 Sansome Street
    San Francisco, CA 94104-1342

FOR SUBSCRIPTION SALES OUTSIDE OF THE UNITED STATES, CONTACT:
    any international subscription agency or Jossey-Bass directly.

OTHER TITLES AVAILABLE IN THE
NEW DIRECTIONS FOR TEACHING AND LEARNING SERIES
Robert J. Menges, Editor-in-Chief
Marilla D. Svinicki, Associate Editor